Reasonable Adjustments
for Autistic Children

Also by Dr Luke Beardon

Autism in Adults
Autism in Childhood: For Parents and Carers of the Newly Diagnosed
Avoiding Anxiety in Autistic Children: A Guide for Autistic Wellbeing
Avoiding Anxiety in Autistic Adults: A Guide for Autistic Wellbeing
What Works for Autistic Children
What Works for Autistic Adults

Reasonable Adjustments for Autistic Children

DR LUKE BEARDON

First published by Sheldon Press in 2024
An imprint of John Murray Press

1

A CIP catalogue record for this title is available from the British Library

Trade Paperback ISBN 9781399815956
ebook ISBN 9781399815963

Typeset by KnowledgeWorks Global Ltd.

Printed and bound in Great Britain by Clays Ltd, Elcograf S.p.A.

John Murray Press policy is to use papers that are natural, renewable and
recyclable products and made from wood grown in sustainable forests.
The logging and manufacturing processes are expected to conform to the
environmental regulations of the country of origin.

John Murray Press   Sheldon Press
Carmelite House   123 S. Broad St., Ste 2750
50 Victoria Embankment   Philadelphia, PA 19109
London EC4Y 0DZ

The authorised representative in the EEA is Hachette Ireland, 8 Castlecourt Centre,
Dublin 15, D15 XTP3, Ireland (email: info@hbgi.ie)

www.sheldonpress.co.uk

John Murray Press, part of Hodder & Stoughton Limited
An Hachette UK company

Dedicated to three sisters, each so beautiful in their own right and all of whom have taught me much about inclusion.

Yvonne, Ems, Han – you mean the world to me, thank you for all you do and for letting me be such a big part of your lives. I love you all.

Contents

Contents

1

What is reasonable?

*All my life, I've been compromised, discriminated against,
made to feel inferior, lesser – wrong. I've had to put
up with slights against my character, been passed over
at work with promotions going to less worthy folk,
and my education caused me too much trauma to even
contemplate. I've been gaslit constantly, I've suffered
with my mental health, I've had to sit by while injustice
after injustice waves over me. I've had to endure physical
pain, bullying, rejection. My life has been one battle after
another, but nothing has really changed. And why? Just
because I'm autistic. Is that reasonable?*

Let's break it down:

*I've been compromised. So – I've never been able to
explore my boundaries. From a very young age, I was told
not to ask stupid questions, not to read what I wanted to
read, not to go off on my own to explore. My reality was
that my questions were genuine, reading user manuals
alongside works of fiction for me was a joy, and autodidactic
learning in solitude really was the only way for me to learn.*

*I've been discriminated against. This one is almost
endless – in fact, I suspect it will only end when I do. At
almost every step of the way, just because I come across
as 'different', I've been a 'problem'. This is the issue – it's
always me that's the problem, and it's always down to me
to 'put it right'. This takes so much energy, so much time
and resource that I am often left behind, disadvantaged –
discriminated against. No one makes the effort to*

understand that my way of doing things might be better for me; it's inevitably a case of 'do it our way or get lost'.

Made to feel inferior, lesser – wrong. It took me decades to even realize that being constantly made to feel this was not, in fact, a common experience among humans. It was only in conversations with like-minded (and like-experienced) individuals that I realized that being made to feel like I was a lesser human being – just for being wired that way – is not ok. That the near-constant belittling and furtive looks, the ignoring of pleas to respond to my requests, the overt comments at how I was always doing things wrong, were not everyday occurrences for most people – and, most importantly, that I am ok as I am; I am not a lesser human, I'm just different.

Slights against my character. My authentic way of being has been covered up to the point that, at times in my life, I just don't know who I am any longer. The need to hide – the desire to be invisible – all stem from those nasty comments about how I should behave differently, better, the same as everyone else. No one else seemed to like me the way I am – to the point that even I disliked myself.

Passed over at work. So many promotional opportunities missed, so many folk that I had helped along their career pathways getting promoted over me. 'You're not a team player,' they say – every time. And yet, in my own way, I am a brilliant team player. Give me a one-on-one opportunity to help others and I am your person, just ask them. More than one and I crumple. But why can't my skills supporting individuals be deemed beneficial to a wider team? What is it they want from me?

Educational trauma. I can't recount this to you in detail as I just want to bury it deep, deep, deep inside, never to see the light of day ever again. I'm told I need to confront my past to be able to live with it, but it's simply

*too painful. Being the one who is made to feel 'other'
as a vulnerable child by peers and adults is too much to
bear. And yet bear it I must, because that was my reality
growing up.*

*Being gaslit – with its effect on my mental health.
Trust me, I don't think many people can experience the
level of their realities being questioned almost on a daily
basis without it impacting on their mental health. Being
told that 'you don't really mean that' or 'that's not true'
or 'it didn't happen that way, you're just paranoid' …
All of these things add up, and add up, and add up. It's
not good.*

*Injustice after injustice. These can be little things with
a huge impact, or big things with a huge impact. For
someone who finds injustice unbearable, it is exquisitely
painful to have to live with injustices being done to me
time and time again. The accusations of lying when I know
I am right, the accusations of being deliberately rude when
I am just trying to help, the accusations of being obstructive
when I am doing my best to be the opposite. No one else
seems to care. I lie awake, night after night, in pain at the
injustice of it all.*

*Pain. Another one which took me years to understand –
that it's not 'normal' to suffer pain from the sensory world,
and that there are sometimes things that can be done
about it. Why didn't anyone tell me? Why did I have to
suffer for all those years, needlessly?*

*Bullying. I don't even think that they mean to be like
that. I think that they believe that it's 'just banter', or 'just
a bit of fun'. Well, not to me it isn't. It's very real, very
dark and very harmful.*

*Rejection. This is the one that really gets me; I try so
hard to be a good person, I try so hard to be the helpful
one, the one who is oh so willing to go over and above to*

make other people's lives better. And yet time and time again, I am made to feel rejected, worthless, and simply 'not right'. For far too long, I've had to battle against who I am, against the 'system', against the way that everyone else does things. It's exhausting.

And why is all of the above my experience? Because I'm autistic, because I didn't know I was for so long, and because others didn't take it into account.

Is that reasonable?

- All autism-related surveys (or similar) include multiple options for how one identifies
- Language/terms within the autism field should be led by the autistic community in all autism-related narratives; or, a clear rationale for not doing so is included as a caveat
- It is an expectation that all practice seriously considers the potential long-term damage to an individual and ensures that everything practicable is done to reduce risk
- The Equality Act recognizes that action/inaction can lead to substantial disadvantage at any point in a person's life – now or in the future – and that this must be taken into account when considering reasonable adjustments
- Avoid disbelieving the autistic voice whenever possible
- Have a belief system that accepts the authentic autistic experience

Terminology

I always suggest to my students that they make sure they are clear as to what terms they will use and why; in particular, I ask them to identify who they mean by 'you' or 'we'.

However, for this book, I am being far more lax in relation to the terms I will be using to allow for flexibility for the reader. I may use 'we' to relate to society as a whole; I may use the colloquial 'you' to essentially mean anyone in general and no one in particular. Far too many texts about autistic people still other the person (i.e. see individuals differently, often in a negative way) by identifying autism to denote the autistic population but not having the same 'standard' to identify the non-autistic population. My aim is to redress this balance by sometimes referring to autistic individuals (usually for emphasis or clarification) and sometimes referring to what I term the predominant neurotype, initialized to PNT. The PNT, as the term suggests, is a non-judgemental, demographically led term to denote a population who hold the majority in terms of their neurotype within any particular context. Obviously, in the main, the PNT would be non-autistic – but this won't always be the case. For example, in a family in which parents and children are all autistic, the PNT in that environment would be autistic.

Just a quick one on terminology and respect. I have certainly changed the way in which I use terminology and language in relation to the autism field over the years, and I fully support the notion that language preferences change over time. What I don't subscribe to, and this will certainly be leading onto a suggested reasonable adjustment, is that the language preferences in the main are led by the so-called professional community, not the autistic community. And another quick one (within the quick one!) as regards terms: by autistic community, I am referring to autistic people; by autism community, I refer to anyone (including the autistic community) who is involved in autism – for example, parents and professionals. While there are obvious Venn-diagram-type overlaps, the two are not one and the same thing. Actually, this does bring me onto something else that could also develop into a reasonable adjustment, and that is the 'drop-down' list of how one might identify when filling in surveys or similar. I get absolutely enraged when there is not the option of multiple answers – see this as an example:

Are you:

- An autistic person
- A parent
- A carer
- A health professional
- An educational professional.

I won't carry on with the list – you get the gist. On the face of it there is nothing wrong with the list – unless you then take into account that I am only 'allowed' to choose one!!! This is a disgrace, and essentially insinuates that one can't be, for example, an autistic professional. So, a suggestion for a reasonable adjustment:

All autism-related surveys (or similar) include multiple options for how one identifies

This may seem excessive when considered a reasonable adjustment – as might several other 'options' littered throughout the book. My argument consistently and continually is that individually at times, and collectively on an ongoing basis, each of these adjustments has the power to decrease substantial disadvantages for the autistic person and could be considered reasonable in relation to implementation. What message does it give to an autistic person, in a not-so-subtle way, that they can *only* be defined as autistic? That they *cannot* be seen as an autistic doctor, or an autistic head teacher? The message – deliberate or otherwise – is that being autistic *precludes* all of these other identities. Not only is this laughably untrue, but also it is offensive in the extreme. This kind of seemingly minor, ongoing, relentless message of 'lesser' absolutely has the power to seriously disadvantage autistic individuals, which is why

I believe that we need to treat reasonable adjustments far more seriously than is currently the case.

Anyway, back to my original point. There is much debate in the autism field around what terms should be used – for example, person-first (child with autism) and identity-first (autistic child) (and I will be going into greater detail about autism-specific terms in a later chapter). Most people will have their preferences (acknowledging that there is a group of (autistic) individuals who are ambivalent), and many who have a preference will express a *strong* preference. Currently, the main preference within the autistic community is for identity-first language to be used, which I absolutely subscribe to. The main reasoning is that autism is an inherent part of one's identity rather than something to be viewed almost separately, as an 'add-on'. There is plenty of writing about the differences of opinions, but my suggestion for a reasonable adjustment is:

Language/terms within the autism field should be led by the autistic community in all autism-related narratives; or, a clear rationale for not doing so is included as a caveat

This seems to me to be, at the very least, courteous, seeing as those narratives are about the autistic population and, therefore, they should have a significant say in how they wish to be represented. Even having a section on terminology with a rationale as to why it has been chosen allows for a level of transparency that is often missing. Narratives will include, for example:

- Any book related to autism
- Autism policies in school or work
- Autism-related research
- Government-led narratives (including policy)
- Health-related works
- Social care writing.

(NB, this is not an exhaustive list.)

Lastly in this terminology section, I will explain how the reasonable adjustments 'system' within the book works. I am no lawyer, nor am I an expert on the Equality Act or any other relevant legislation. I cannot offer suggestions of adjustments that can subsequently be deemed as a lawful requirement. What I can do is provide examples of what I believe to be at least potential reasonable adjustments alongside a rationale as to why I believe that to be the case. All of my reasoning, explicit or implicit, is based on three intertwined components – the concept of reasonable, the concept of substantial disadvantage, and autism. All of the suggestions are included as bullet points at the start of each chapter for ease of use, and within the text, they are all presented as stand-alone text in bold to make them stand out.

I have also included several examples, which are presented in italics, of how adjustments might make a difference in real-life practice.

So – within the context of this book, what are these suggestions that are in bold and italics? They are categorically not (currently) legally required reasonable adjustments that require implementation. However, in my view they are what might be taken into consideration when trying to work out what a reasonable adjustment looks like. I don't have the power – but if I did, I would implement every single one of them to be enshrined in law, and I fully believe that this would be positively impactful on the lives of autistic people. I have tried to provide a rationale for each one to 'show my workings out', but, essentially, I have aimed to do the best I can to provide suggestions that, within the Equality Act, appear to me to be at least worthy of considering whether they meet the criteria.

What the Equality Act states

Right – so, this is the slightly technical bit about what the law states and why we should be acting on it. The Act I am referring to is the Equality Act 2010, which was passed to legally protect people from discrimination, harassment or victimization at work, in school and in wider society. It covers protected characteristics such as age, disability, marriage, pregnancy and maternity, race, religion or belief, sexual identity and orientation. I will go on to 'discuss' the concepts of what actually constitutes 'reasonable' and 'substantial' which are key to the actual legislation – and the whole premise of this book is to create a narrative which explores what changes could be made to better the lives of autistic children.

The Act itself, in principle, is wonderful – arguably *any* legislation that seeks to reduce any kind of discrimination should be applauded. However, there is often a stark disparity between what *should* be lawfully done and what is *actually* done in reality. It could also be argued that some of the terminology involved is problematic, as there is no definitive way of understanding terms – as is so often in law, there are different interpretations, so subjectivity will always play a part. For the purposes of clarity, I will identify what my 'interpretation' is and what I feel should be taken into account when ascertaining when reasonable adjustments should be implemented, alongside a brief explanation of the Act (in relation to autism).

The simplest component of the Act in relation to autism is to answer the question – is autism covered under the Act? And the answer is yes. Irrespective of whether you believe autism to be a disability, being autistic means that the Act can be drawn upon in relation to an individual being autistic. Autism is classified (under the Act) as a disability, and disability is what is included explicitly under the Act.

Duty to make reasonable adjustments

There is a duty for organizations providing public services to make reasonable adjustments under the Act to ensure that autistic individuals are not discriminated against. But what does this actually mean?

What is 'reasonable'?

The answer to this question is: your autism – so, as noted, this is a simple one. If you are autistic, then you are covered by the Act. The Act clearly identifies autism (it actually refers to 'Autistic Spectrum Disorders') as a disability arising from a set of impairments. Quite aside from the pejorative terminology which I vehemently disagree with, the end result is that being autistic means that one is covered by the Act. Or does it? The question is what does it mean to be autistic – in other words, does one have to have a formal diagnosis in order to 'qualify' for reasonable adjustments. The answer appears to be no – but I cannot find anything within the Act about formal diagnosis. There seems to be consensus that while a formal diagnosis may not be a necessity, there may be a requirement to provide 'medical evidence' of 'an impairment' when considering the Act. My take on this is that if there is any conflict (e.g. a tribunal) then medical evidence of impairment may be required.

What is 'substantial'?

Another term within the Act that is open to interpretation is whether an individual can be considered to be at a *substantial* disadvantage if no adjustments are made. I take issue with this for three reasons:

1 Why should you be at *any* disadvantage, let alone a substantial one for being autistic?
2 How is substantial understood in relational terms?

3 Who is deciding what is substantial or otherwise – is the autistic lens being taken into account?

My first point above is perhaps a slightly over-zealous one – however, autistic children have been at such a disadvantage in so many areas of life for so long it seems unfair or harsh to me that there is a seemingly acceptable concept that it's ok to be disadvantaged in any manner at all. Until society seeks to redress the unfair imbalance of privilege, then autistic people will continue to be treated as second-class citizens. It's the principle here that is objectionable rather than the law itself. In a genuinely equitable society, *no one* should be discriminated against or be disadvantaged as a result of their minority status.

The second point is an essential component in the process of understanding discrimination. The 'relational' terminology is very deliberate – I am referring to the notion that relatedness is important when understanding impact; for example, one might argue that a misunderstanding at school over what homework constitutes because of an ambiguity in instructions won't cause substantial disadvantage to a student. However, if we begin to understand the relatedness of suffering ambiguity of homework instruction to a longer-term impact on mental wellbeing, then we may feel somewhat differently.

> *It all started when I was asked to write about my understanding of the galaxy. As it happens, at that particular time, I was absolutely captivated by The Hitchhiker's Guide to the Galaxy, so I enthusiastically wrote reams about the wonderful narrative and a review of the book. I was told in no uncertain terms a few days later that I had deliberately chosen to misinterpret the instructions and that I had to stay behind at school to complete the 'correct' homework. I didn't realize at the time, but this incident was to cast a shadow over me for years to come. For so long I was terrified about following*

11

instructions, to the point that I used to point-blank refuse, which then led to all sorts of correspondence with my parents about how disobedient I was – even leading at one point to a temporary exclusion. The problem wasn't that I couldn't understand what had gone wrong – once it was explained to me, I could see the funny side, although I was still annoyed that my perspective wasn't listened to. No, the real issue was that the teacher refused to accept any responsibility, and I was the one who was punished – totally unfairly, in my view. I lost faith in the school system and every time I was asked to follow instructions, I had this absolute fear and mental block; I simply couldn't do it. No one believed me when I tried to explain how it was related to the galaxy incident; no one wanted to hear my voice, no one was on my side. Which meant that every single time something like this happened, I felt even worse than the last time – it was like I was being punished over and over again, each time worse than before – when I don't think I should have been punished in the first instance. For someone who has a very strong sense of fairness, this sent me into a spiral of decline that I think will affect me in a negative way for the rest of my life. All they had to do was accept they might have made a small mistake and agreed with me that I had made a valiant attempt to do my homework properly. Was that too much to ask?

It is imperative to buy into the fact that being at a substantial disadvantage can come into effect at any age. Just because one's PTSD (Post Traumatic Stress Disorder) isn't evident until years later in no way detracts from the significance of the event(s) that caused it. Of course, there is no way of knowing what the future might hold, but at the very least we need to be doing everything we can to reduce risk of trauma. This might sound obvious, but in reality, how much time and effort is taken around considering reasonable adjustments in relation to reducing potential impact of substantial disadvantage years down the line? And yet, it is very clear on speaking with autistic adults that some of their substantial disadvantages in life stem directly from their experiences as children. Therefore, a suggestion:

It is an expectation that all practice seriously considers the potential long-term damage to an individual and ensures that everything practicable is done to reduce risk

'All practice' is quite the all-encompassing phrase, but it is meant seriously. Being autistic does not come and go depending on the situation in which you find yourself. It is an intrinsic part of who a person is. Therefore, all engagement with an individual needs to take autism into account. Some folk might argue against this, querying reasons such as 'why should autistic children be any different from anyone else?' Well, the clue is in their own words. Autistic children are, *by definition*, different from the PNT; therefore, practice is surely more likely to need to be adapted to meet need. Other differences in life are much easier for society to understand. Under the Equality Act, no one would seriously refuse a wheelchair user the use of a ramp. In my mind, it is the need that is important, not necessarily where that need comes from. So, if there is an 'autistic need', then that is just as important as a ramp. Just because one need is perhaps more obvious than another doesn't make the less obvious any less of a need. The recent increase in signage relating to what might be less apparent is a wonderful example of progression; for example, 'not all disabilities are obvious or can be seen' or similar. I'm not suggesting that autism is automatically a disability, but I am noting that such narratives are a very welcome reminder that some needs are not always obvious.

The example above leads on to the third point – who is making the decisions, and are they able to do so taking the autism lens into account? This goes all the way back to my earlier point about empathy, which is discussed in my previous book *What Works for Autistic Adults*: if we accept that there are many individuals who lack the ability to genuinely empathize with autistic people – and are unable, for whatever reason, to properly listen and take the individual seriously and understand the potential for impact – then what hope is there for a decision to be made that is appropriate to the circumstances? In fact, could it even be argued that unless there are individuals involved in the decision-making process who are able to display autistic empathy, then that process itself could, potentially, be unlawful? In other words, might autistic children be at a substantial disadvantage without the adjustment of including autistic-empathic personnel as part of decision-making? Take an employment tribunal as an example:

> It is clear to me that I was unfairly treated at work, which led to me being dismissed. I was so frustrated – time and time again, I asked my employer to stop calling me into meetings with him without any warning. My brain simply won't work at that short notice; I can't switch from doing my job to talking to my line manager without preparation. All I needed was 15 minutes' warning with a very brief email articulating what it was he wanted to talk about. He just ignored me, over and over again.
>
> So I took them to a tribunal. My worry with the tribunal was that because I am so intelligent and articulate, then the same judgement would be made, as it so often is – that if I'm that bright, then I can't possibly have an issue with talking to my line manager about work, within a work setting, without advance warning. Maybe it's the case that only someone else similar to me would really

> *appreciate how impossible it is and would then rule in my*
> *favour – but how many people like that are likely to be*
> *part of the tribunal?*

By 'substantial', the Act means that it should not be minor or trivial. Again, these are subjective terms that need to be understood through the autistic lens and/or with autistic empathy, otherwise the risk is that what might appear minor or trivial to the PNT may for the autistic person be anything but.

Take the following example of what I've been told on many occasions:

> *I've been told time and time again that it's such a trivial*
> *thing, and for me 'not to worry about it'. But to me, it's*
> *not trivial – in fact, to me, it's incredibly important. And*
> *the fact that no one else seems to care alongside the*
> *fact that I am constantly being made to feel stupid just*
> *because everyone else finds it trivial makes it even worse.*
> *No one actually seems to understand just how devastating*
> *being told this actually is – just because to them it doesn't*
> *cause any concern. But why can't they realize that I am not*
> *them? That to me that thing is not only important, but*
> *massively impactful?*

I've deliberately not included what the so-called triviality is in the example because it is, by definition, so individual. The principle, though, is essential to take on board – just because most people might find something trivial does not mean that it can't have a substantial impact on someone else.

The following factors can also be considered when it comes to the decision-making process as to whether an adjustment should be made – in other words, influences whether the adjustment is deemed as reasonable. There are plenty of online resources explaining these points further:

- Practicability
- Will the changes make a difference?
- Size of organization
- How much resource (including money) is available
- How much changes cost
- Whether changes have already been made.

What the Act states needs to be done

There are three areas in which the Act identifies the potential need for adjustments. These are: changes in the things that are done, the physical environment and the provision of aids or services.

There is a duty to change the way things are done (e.g. policy, process, rule) in practice; here is an example:

Case study: School uniform policy

A school has a rigid school uniform policy, but there has been a pupil identified who has sensory needs that suggest that she finds the specific material of the uniform uncomfortable to the point of distraction. In this case, there are two key elements to consider: 1. if no adjustment is made, would the pupil be at a substantial disadvantage, and 2. would it be reasonable for the school to alter their policy to reduce risk of discrimination to the pupil?

If the argument is that being distracted means that the pupil's education is compromised – which is certainly the case for many students with sensory needs – then yes, there is a good case to suggest that without adjustments the pupil would be at a substantial disadvantage as her education could suffer. If the school made changes to the school uniform policy to provide a range of options (including alternative materials of clothing), would this be regarded as 'reasonable'? Again, my view is that the answer should be 'yes'. The adjustment:

- is practicable
- will make a difference
- doesn't take up many (or any) resources, including financial ones.

There is a duty to change the physical environment. Here is an example:

Case study: Toilets at work

It has been brought to the attention of an employer that the sensory needs of an autistic employee are such that they cannot currently access the staff toilets. Specifically, the soap dispensers are extremely pungent, and this causes physical pain to the employee who has noted that they have hyperosmia. This culminates in the employee having to leave work each time they need to use the toilet in order to access other facilities in town with a more neutral-smelling soap. In this case, it should be fairly apparent that the employer should simply change the soap in the facilities in order to reduce the risk of the employee being at a substantial disadvantage. Again, the adjustment:

- is practicable
- will make a difference
- doesn't take up many (or any) resources including financial ones.

There is a duty to provide extra aids or services. Here is an example:

Case study: Providing information in a different format

A university student finds it very difficult to process written information in the feedback he gets on his draft work, and is aware that there are alternatives that he finds much easier to process. In fact, he has gone to great lengths to time his processing speeds between written/visual feedback and audio feedback, and can demonstrate that his brain takes five times longer to process visual feedback compared to audio. His argument is that he should be entitled to audio feedback over visual feedback as otherwise it puts him at a substantial disadvantage compared to his peers. In this case, again, there is no resource implication to the university as there is free software available to create audio feedback; it doesn't take the lecturer any longer to provide feedback in this way; and the student would be at a substantial disadvantage if the change were not implemented.

Outcomes of reasonable adjustments (what happens if not provided and potential of implementation)

The potential impact of the Act cannot be underestimated. If implemented properly, it can have an extraordinary impact – and, conversely, lack of appropriate application can have devastating consequences. Taking this point into account, we simply cannot ignore the relational components of the domino effect of not applying the Act in a way to suit the autistic individual. One thing *does* lead to another – and another – and, if the end result is a substantial disadvantage, then we really need to do something about it. One of the major problems in relation to the Equality Act is the grey nature and subjectivity around how one decides whether or not a child is at a substantial disadvantage. One of the critical questions that requires posing here – in my mind – is *when in the child's life are they at a substantial disadvantage?* All too often, it would appear that there is a time limitation that is all too brief when it comes to the notion of substantial disadvantage. In other words, there is often a lack of what substantial disadvantage might look like in years to come – as opposed to the immediate future. Chapter 2 will go on to discuss the implications of microaggressions, but for the time being consider the following example:

> *Matt is a 54-year-old individual who cannot apply for any job where it is indicated that he would need to be subjected to an interview in order to be assessed for the job. Matt is a capable individual and would/could make for a very effective employee, but all but 10 per cent of the jobs available for him to apply for also come with an interview. Is Matt at a substantial disadvantage by not being able to apply for those other 90 per cent of jobs – only in effect being able to apply for 10 per cent of jobs overall? I would suggest that the answer is yes.*
>
> *The reason why Matt is unable to apply for jobs that come with an interview is because he suffers tremendously from the trauma at being put on the spot and questioned by those who he feels are in authority. This stems from the fact that Matt was so frequently asked at school to stand up in front of the class to answer questions from the person in authority at the time – the teacher – and this caused him so much anxiety that it has led to current*

day, ongoing trauma and it means he is unable to even contemplate having to succumb to being exposed to an interview.

Now, the issue implied in this scenario – which is by no means uncommon – is that who in the current climate really takes into account what impact practice for a child today might have on that child decades in the future? Does the Act explicitly state that we need to consider whether that child might be at a substantial disadvantage – not just in the here and now, but in the longer-term future as an adult? As the answer is no, might the Act itself require a reasonable adjustment to its own legislation? How about this as a suggestion:

The Equality Act recognizes that action/inaction can lead to substantial disadvantage at any point in a person's life – now or in the future – and that this must be taken into account when considering reasonable adjustments

Exploration of autism and why adjustments might need to be made

The précis at the start of the chapter is just one example of why being autistic can be so disadvantageous in life when adjustments to/for that child are not considered nor implemented. Quite simply, ignoring a person being autistic is likely to dramatically increase risk to that person's wellbeing. In some cases, the lack of adjustments can result in severely compromising situations – never underestimate the impact of inaction! In fact, I genuinely believe that so much of the distress that is suffered by autistic children has nothing to do with any malicious intent; rather, it is quite simply a lack of appreciation as to the impact that behaviour and/or lack of adjustments (or, even, inappropriate adjustments) can have on the autistic population/person. I also believe that this might have something to do with empathy – or, lack of.

I've written previously about empathy in my book *What Works for Autistic Adults* and how difficult it can be for the PNT to empathize with autistic individuals, and I suspect this might be at the heart of many of the problems that are faced daily by autistic children. But is it reasonable to assume that lack of empathy should lead to lack of action? 'Simply' not understanding the issue is not a good enough excuse to do nothing about it. One of the simplest, and yet one of the least common experiences of autistic people, is *simply being believed*. Why is it that so many autistic people report that when they try to explain what life is like for them, what they feel might be beneficial as an adjustment and what impact it might have, they are just met with disbelief? I don't for one moment think that the reaction of disbelief is always one of malicious intent, but I do suspect that it stems from a lack of empathic understanding – a lack of shared experience. Perhaps this should be the most obvious reasonable adjustment of all, and maybe if this were implemented (at no financial cost whatsoever) then a lot of the damaging impact of being autistic in a non-compromising world would be alleviated. The suggested reasonable adjustment being: believe the autistic child, even if you don't share their experience. Actually, what might be even better than this – believe the autistic child, *especially* if you don't share their experience. I've found that populations can be split into three when reacting to an autistic child trying to explain their experiences:

1 Rejection
2 Acceptance
3 Interest.

Allow me to explain with a personal example. I have a very real difficulty in recognizing people – some refer to this as face blindness or, to give it a diagnostic term, prosopagnosia. Over the years, I have tried to explain this to people and have come across each of the three reactions identified above. Rejection is when people simply don't believe me. This isn't usually in an overt 'you're lying' response, but is hurtful, nonetheless. Comments such as 'It can't be that difficult' or 'I'm sure you can recognize people better than you're making out' or even 'Well, I've not come across that before, is it really a thing?' all insinuate that I am somehow making it up, and the notion is being rejected despite the fact I am being open and honest. (By the way, it is a very real thing and can have many unintended consequences, trust me!!!).

The second reaction, acceptance, is almost always when the person with whom I am engaging also experiences the same phenomena. This usually precipitates the sharing of experiences and is often a delightful and rare experience of mutual understanding. It can also give rise to quite a hilarious 'who has got into the most awkward situation?' type of conversation – again, sharing these experiences with like-minded folk can be extraordinarily sublime.

The third reaction, interest, comes when the individual doesn't empathize but does believe – and is interested in an honest discussion as to what it feels like, and even if there is anything they can do in the way of support. (Hint: if I recognize you by your hairstyle/hair colour, then your visit to the hairdresser is likely to mean I won't know who you are; a gentle non-judgemental reminder as to who you are – and the context in which I know you – the next time we meet is all that is required, thank you).

Self-indulgence aside, taking my example and extrapolating it to the autistic experience gives an indication as to why it is so important to listen to the autistic perspective and believe that the lived autistic experience is an authentic one, even if it doesn't align to your own experiences. So, my suggestion for a reasonable adjustment is:

Avoid disbelieving the autistic voice whenever possible

And the next is:

Have a belief system that accepts the authentic autistic experience

Simply having belief in an autistic child's narrative can go an awfully long way towards reducing risk of discrimination against them. I write about epistemic injustice in later chapters, but this is a pertinent opportunity to bring in the concept of testimonial injustice as part of the argument for believing autistic people. Testimonial injustice in relation to autism is, essentially, not believing the autistic child as a direct result of them being autistic. There are other types of testimonial injustice – for example, based on sex or race – but in this instance, I am referring to autistic children being seen as less credible simply as a result of being themselves. One of the most important aspects of this is the lack of belief in one's lived experience – how it really is for you, as opposed to how other people choose to believe it is for you. This will be a theme throughout the book because it is so heavily influential in how autistic children are understood and subsequently engaged with.

While I am on the subject of believing in the authentic autistic experience, it's worth pointing out the damage that is done by constantly having to somehow 'prove' that what one is saying is actually true. Imagine what your life would be like if every time you told someone something about yourself, they rejected your experience as if it were invalid? And then imagine the joy of discovering someone who actually took the time to listen to you, accepted what you said as true and acted upon it with your advice. It makes a tremendous difference to quality of life – so as a reasonable adjustment, surely belief is a no-brainer?

Going all the way back to the title of the chapter – 'what is reasonable?' – and having completed the chapter (nearly), I can only conclude that it was right to attempt the writing of this book. As I write, I am reminded of more and more autistic children that I know of who fundamentally are not having their needs met, many of which could be considered as a right under the Equality Act. Is it reasonable to expect autistic children to continue being discriminated against by society not implementing reasonable 'reasonable adjustments'? I don't think so.

2

Society

> - The more negative society is about autism, the greater the risk there is to autistic wellbeing
> - Society accepts autism – and, by extension, autistic people – as an expected and welcome part of humankind
> - Cures for autism are soundly rejected
> - Schools should add autism and other neurodivergences to the curriculum alongside more common topics of teaching around minority groups such as race and gender
> - All misinformation about autism is valid checked by an autistic-led authoritative body

Society – in whatever form it takes for you – will have an impact, almost invariably, on how autism is understood. This, in turn, will have an influence – directly and/or indirectly – on how autistic people are viewed. A simple equation might be:

The more negative society is about autism, the greater the risk there is to autistic wellbeing

You may well retort with a 'so what?' – what does this have to do with reasonable adjustments? Well, my perspective is that we – as a society – need to take far greater responsibility for our concepts, language and practice when it comes to autism as a reasonable adjustment (or series of reasonable adjustments) in and of itself. It would be very difficult to somehow understand society as a whole organization that can be held to account under the Equality Act. I can and must accept that. But – are there organizations that form components of society that *could* (and should) be held to account *that are influenced by more global concepts from society as a whole*? Presumably, the answer is yes. If this is the case, then, addressing some of the root causes of discrimination at a societal level – while still holding organizations and institutions to account – seems to be a sensible way forward.

Going back to the above equation, one might be forgiven for thinking that society in its global sense can't really have that much influence over one person. This is a dangerous perspective and one fraught with difficulty. In fact, I would go as far as to suggest that the opposite is the case. It is the ongoing exposure to the sometimes subtle negativity surrounding autism that can lead to very negative individual practice that can and does lead to a decline in a child's wellbeing. That is what this chapter is all about.

By 'society', I refer to a group of individuals living together in an organized way, with a similar set of rules; there are many different ways in which this could be interpreted, from a UK- or American-wide society at a macro level, down to more of a community at a smaller level. In a sense, definitions here are less relevant than the concepts themselves. The reality is that if a societal concept/attitude/philosophy leads to autistic distress then something needs to be done about it. Once the cause of the issue has been highlighted, only then can we identify which aspect of society needs addressing. For example, one might regard a school in its own right as a kind of mini-society, and identify that the school's policy on inclusion is actually discriminatory – in which case, it's the school that needs attention. Often, in relation to the ideas in this chapter, it is less obvious as to the who or what is to be held to account; this in no way detracts from the necessity for change.

Make no mistake – society/societies have an abundant power over how we develop an understanding (or misunderstanding) of autism. Say, for example, I am interested in finding out more about autism – what do I do? As with almost every other member of my society, I 'Google' it. Just think about that for a moment in terms of how society can be influenced. Google didn't exist as a search engine until 1998 – just a mere eight years later 'to google' was recognized in major dictionaries as a transitive verb. It is now extremely common to use this kind of language in reference to searching on the internet – which is an example of just how powerful society can be over a short period of time.

Anyway, back to the point – after doing my search on 'what is autism?' and clicking on the images button, I have a page of information relating to a search engine's identification of images related to those search terms. As of April 2024, the first page of images included the following terms:

- Disorder
- Signs
- Symptoms
- Challenges
- Problems
- Levels
- Trouble
- Rigid
- Inflexible
- inappropriate
- Inability
- Poor
- Strange
- Difficulty
- Issues
- Eccentric.

By first page, I refer to the nine 'top' images that appeared. Not all the narrative was quite so negative, but terms such as 'difference' as opposed to 'disorder' or 'difficulty' were very much in the minority. Just a quick flick through the bullet points above is a convenient snapshot as to what might be met by someone wanting to find out more about autism and demonstrates, at least partially, what kind of narrative society associates with autism. This level of negativity is subsequently hugely influential over how society views autism – but, even more worrying, how a parent might view their child or, how an autistic child might view themselves.

Concepts – language – practice (general)

I've broken down societal influence into three components – concepts, language, and practice (in general – more specific practice is covered in later chapters). I'm sure that this is by no means exhaustive, and there are plenty of other areas that require attention; however, these are three of the key components that I believe lead to autistic suffering – often needlessly – as a result of societal influence. It will be crystal clear to those in the know reading this chapter that I am leaning very heavily on other authors – there is no way that I can take credit for some of the superb work led by the autistic community.

Concepts
Ethnocentric and neuronormativity

Ethnocentricity plays its part in the debates around the conceptual understanding of autism, but neuronormativity is perhaps a more useful autism-linked term that wonderfully explains what an inherent issue this is within communities. 'Ethnocentricity' refers to the concept that a people may have a lack of respect for other cultures or peoples – that their own way of being, their nationality, their culture is somehow better than others. This can cover a wide range of 'peoples' and cultures and, in the case of this chapter, one could promote the idea within ethnocentricity that autistic populations are being seen as 'lesser' than the PNT. However, I feel that ethnocentricity at least implies some level of overt consciousness that is presumably unfair if that is not the case. The whole purpose of this chapter is to identify society and societal concepts that are harming autistic children – not individuals themselves per se. Neuronormativity is less about culture and more about existence; that there is a 'right' way of functioning within communities and, therefore, a *less* desirable way of being, thinking or acting. Neuronormativity refers to how society has an expectation of norm – including development – that is a preferred option, and that to deviate from that norm is inherently problematic. This automatically places autism in a negative category – currently, autism is clearly positioned in relative terms; in other words, relative to the perceived norm. Autistic children are defined as being deficient in certain areas in relation to the 'norm'. Therefore, from the outset, autism is rooted in problematic discourse that positions the autistic person as less desirable than the norm.

The grief model is perhaps the most obvious narrative that positions autism as something reprehensible to be avoided almost at all costs. Possibly outdated – I would hope – but still sometimes referred to, the model suggests to parents of a newly identified autistic child that they can expect to go through a grieving process, and that it's perfectly understandable and acceptable to relate the child's autism identification with a bereavement. I am being deliberately extreme in writing this – but trust me, I have many examples of exactly this narrative being presented to parents by professionals. This model suggests that it is so terrible to have an autistic child – as opposed, presumably, to a 'normal' child (whatever that means) – that it is akin to being bereaved. That being autistic is so terrible that the parent will actually grieve the child that they would or could have had in place of the current autistic one. Even writing this gives me shivers. While this is an extreme form of discourse that highlights the neuronormativity paradigm effectively, it doesn't mean for one moment that less extreme forms are any less impactful. I would go as far as to suggest that *any* discourse that promotes the idea of autistic equating to lesser can be damaging – indeed, is likely to be damaging.

And yet, again at that conceptual level, autism *is* so very often understood within society in a neuronormative way. Similar to unconscious bias, almost no one will be aware of this – which is problematic in its own right. Until society realizes that their own concept of autism is potentially flawed then we won't be doing much about it. A similar parallel would be decades ago when people didn't realize just how discriminatory their view of ethnic minorities could have been; not that I'm saying it's perfect today, but it's come an awfully long way over the last few decades. But I think society's relationship with autism is far less advanced than its relationship with other groups such as ethnic minorities.

Historically – and don't worry, I am not intending to launch into a history lesson – autism has always been positioned within the academic and medical literature as problematic, so it is no wonder that today's society still situates its own concepts in a similar way. In fact, to this day, so much of the narrative within academia and medical literature still refers to autism as problematic, although that is slowly changing. I'm not trying to make excuses – just trying to establish a baseline for understanding from which we can, hopefully, move forward. Chapter 3 will delve a little more into the medical model of the diagnostic manuals. Suffice to say that, currently, we are a long way off from conceptualizing autism as something that is a natural part of humankind and not something to be seen as inherently negative. A simple (in some ways) suggested adjustment could, therefore, be:

> **Society accepts autism – and, by extension, autistic people – as an expected and welcome part of humankind**

It sounds so simple when presented as such, and yet the fact that for decades, autism has been viewed as a disorder and something to be troubled by suggests that we are a long way from getting there.

Ableism

Ableism is the discrimination against individuals who are deemed to be disabled. And I have made the attempt to identify those three components of discrimination in the following sections. As elsewhere, I am not trying to suggest that individuals are deliberately ableist – in some ways, it might be easier if ableism was a more conscious process as it then becomes less nebulous and more tangible. The fact that, in the main, there is a level of institutionalized ableism in society makes it far more difficult to tackle. The insidious and invidious nature of ableism can make it a problematic beast to tackle; but tackle it we must as part of our duty towards anti-discriminatory practice.

An ableist attitude is one that positions autism automatically as something negative. The ableist narrative at the conceptual level is one that includes suggestions of autism requiring fixing somehow – possibly changing and/or treating or, in the extreme sense, curing. Actually, this isn't the most extreme; the most extreme would be the eugenic position whereby a search for an autism gene subsequently leads to debates about the removal of it from the gene pool for the betterment of humankind. This kind of discourse is worrying to extreme degrees. The very notion that being autistic is so problematic to society that we should be seeking to eradicate autism from the population is seriously extraordinary. I'm never really quite sure whether anyone genuinely seeks to do this; however, there are often stories about scientists seeking for the 'autism gene' or similar. One has to wonder why there is such a search – after all, what would the result be should one be discovered? I am fully aware that the argument is that such a discovery could lead to 'autism tests' that definitively identify individuals as autistic; however, a far more sinister and disturbing notion is that identifying an autism gene could mean a step closer to someone suggesting that removing it might be something that society might want to consider. Imagine a life without autistic people? It doesn't bear thinking about! I hesitate to write a reasonable adjustment about this as, in a sense, it seems to me to be so ludicrous that even drawing attention to it is at the very least distasteful – but we need to be pragmatic. The following is what helped me make my mind up.

I am writing this on 18 April 2024, at 13.47. I have not done as much writing as I had intended, as I was busy crafting a response to a media article that came out in the news this morning. The headline was:

> The Met Police has launched an investigation over concerns about stem-cell injections being offered to children as a cure for autism

And the article went on to write: A spokesperson said the authority had recently been made aware of concerns that 'an individual claiming to be a doctor plans to visit the UK to offer dangerous, experimental procedures on children with autism'.

So, my suggestion:

Cures for autism are soundly rejected

As always, whenever I make such a bold suggestion (or is it bold?) I have to add the caveat that I am well aware of the suffering of autistic children at the hands of a society that does not understand nor support them in a way that suits the population. But, as I have always maintained, these issues are as a result of poor autism acceptance and adaptations within society, not because they, or you, are autistic *per se* – hence the reason for writing this book.

Does there need to be a reasonable adjustment based on the notion of a cure? Well – maybe a less open-ended way would simply be to ascertain whether it meets the criteria. Are autistic children at a substantial disadvantage with people trying to irrevocably alter their very way of being? Would it be reasonable to suggest that this should not be an option? I'll leave that for you to decide. But while you're deciding, just think of those very children alive right now who have read that article. The message that it conveys to them is very clearly that they are in need of a cure, that there is something fundamentally wrong with them. To me, irrespective of the Equality Act, that is simply dehumanizing and potentially devastating.

As it happens, the response to the media was rejected – so I have decided to include it here (one might ask why it was rejected in the first place?):

Stem-Cell Autism Cure – A Response

Sadly, the news today includes an article about how the Met Police are investigating a possible offer of a 'cure' for autism involving stem cell and injections of such into the brain. I won't go into the (pseudo) science behind the proposal – you can read more of it here: <https://www.bbc.co.uk/news/uk-england-london-68759263>

Irrespective of the clearly ludicrous nature of the claim, the reality is that society across the globe is still so inherently ableist in its perspective of autism that such stories are not really that shocking. The fact that there is still a commodification of autism as a potential money-spinner, preying on the vulnerability of parents, has its roots in the concept that autism is a bad thing that *needs* a cure. Without this neuronormative stance which suggests that there is a 'right' way of processing information and communicating, without this constant pressure to normalize and pressurize autistic people to conform, without the constant rhetoric with pejorative terms such as 'disorder', 'impairment', 'problem', 'deficit', perhaps there would be a welcome decrease in society thinking that autism is something that needs to be 'treated' or 'cured'.

I am categorically in no way decrying the very real difficulties faced by autistic people of all ages nor the issues that are also faced by parents; the horrific statistics around autistic mental ill health and suicide speak for themselves. However, my view is that the vast majority of these problems are as a result of society 'getting it wrong' – not as a result of people being autistic per se. Of course, there are all sorts of intersectionality issues that can also be at play – but perhaps that is a different paper.

The point in relation to a response to today's news is the horrifying fact that autism is still perceived, at least by some, as being so terrible that there is even the vaguest mileage in risking a child's life with any 'intervention' in order to eradicate it. This seems to me to be an utterly disgusting concept that totally misconstrues what autistic people themselves present as their lived experiences, needs and wishes. Of course, I am (again categorically) not taking all autistic people's perspectives into account; I am fully aware that some autistic people (and parents of autistic children) feel that 'the autism is to blame' for the very real, often traumatic experiences that autistic individuals have to face. However, if society were to dramatically change its perspective and embrace autism as part of the natural neurodiversity of humankind and welcome autistic people as important (I would say essential) components of the community, then maybe that paradigm shift would go some way towards changing the environment to better suit autistic needs – rather than, as history shows, trying to force autistic people to fit in with everyone else, even when it causes no end of trauma.

A truly autism-inclusive environment could refer to my (self-professed) 'golden equation' of autism + environment = outcome. Accepting that we should *not* be trying to change a person being autistic (to use it a third time – there is categorically no such thing as an 'autism cure'), then if we want to change the outcome for the autistic person then instead of the focus being on autism, it should be on the environment. In simple terms – everyone else.

Better understanding, more engagement with the autistic community, better support systems, creation of a truly inclusive environment in all walks of life, an ongoing proactive emphasis on autistic wellbeing and total rejection of the notion that being autistic is somehow to be 'lesser' is the way forward, not to seek to remove autism either from a person or from the population.

Ableism might not go as far as to suggest that autism is something that needs eradication, but there are numerous examples that can be given around the ableist attitude at the conceptual level that autism is in some way undesirable, or is ignored, or the individual is mistreated based on a concept – three examples are:

What's so special about them?

An overheard conversation at school: 'It does my head in. It's always autism this, autism that. Always the same, always "you've got to change this, you've got to change that". Always the pressure on me to sort out their issues – honestly, I don't see what the problem is, all children need support, why should they be so different? Why should they get special attention?'

We all do it like that

Jess, an autistic child, has not been allowed to bring her iPad into school to complete her work on. The response from the school is that no one else needs an iPad – the assertion being that just because no one else needs one, she doesn't either. In fact, Jess communicated very effectively with her iPad, and very ineffectively if she is forced into communicating in other ways, which cause her intense anxiety.

This example of ableism is based on the attitude that the majority way of doing things should be adopted by everyone; in the autism field, this represses a natural autistic way of doing things and denies the autistic person the right to do things in a way that suits them.

You need to try harder

'Look, it's not that I don't understand that you're autistic. It's just that you need to learn to join the others; otherwise how else are you going to fit in? How else

are you going to learn how to get on with big groups of people? You need to try harder to get on with others rather than taking the easy route all the time. You'll see as you get older, this is all for your own good. You'll thank me one day.'

I think that this example requires additional explanation and breaking down. And by the way – yes, it's a real-life example.

First of all is the reassurance – the acknowledgement that the child, call him Alan, is autistic. Alan likes this – someone has actually identified him in the way that he likes to be identified. But this makes the following narrative that much harder for Alan to take – if the teacher knows that he's autistic, then why is he making these suggestions? Alan has been told that he needs to learn how to join the others – but it's not something that can be learned as such. Alan knows very well how to join a group, but that doesn't detract from the intense sensory pain and social anxiety that comes with it. And nothing will ever change that so far as Alan can tell. What he is certain of is that 'simply' joining in will just be more exposure to the pain. How else is Alan going to fit in? This assumes that Alan does, in fact, want to fit in, which is a dubious perspective. Many autistic individuals are rightly proud of themselves and their own unique way of being, and being told that they have to fit in can be seen as ableist in itself. Even if Alan does want to fit in, being forced to do so in the same way as everyone is definitely an example of ableism with the assumption that one way is the only way. Then there is the assumption that Alan *has* to get on with big groups of people. To my mind this is a misapprehension. It is perfectly possible to thrive in life without being involved in big groups of people. Then there is the dreaded comment about having to try harder. It is literally impossible for Alan to access the group without being in sensory and social pain. Trying not to be in pain doesn't work. If it did, painkillers would cease to be required. It's as simple as that.

Ok – so the above breakdown might seem overly simplistic, so I will acknowledge (or pre-empt) some additional points. Yes, I accept that the teacher is genuine, and wants what is best for Alan. However, he is still doing it from an ableist perspective, thinking that doing things the same as everyone else is the 'right' way forward. There is no concession whatsoever to Alan being autistic. The teacher also believes that Alan must learn to engage with big groups – again, he is doing so for *his* reasons: that he thinks that it will help Alan in the future. If he really understood Alan, then he would realize that, at least for the time being, on balance it would be better for Alan to find an alternative rather than risk the trauma of ongoing pain – which, ironically enough, would put Alan off groups forever.

Internalized ableism

I intend to write much more on this in the next book around the same subject but with the adult population in mind. However, it would be remiss not to at least make mention of internalized ableism and what it means. Internalized ableism, pretty much as the term suggests, is when you unwittingly pick up on ableist attitudes and subsequently have some elements of ableism yourself. This can be directed at others or even yourself. This latter is devastating to see – children who genuinely feel that they are worthless, or 'worth less' than others – simply as a direct result of being autistic. Many autistic young people refute their identification as a direct result of internalized ableism; the notion of being autistic is displeasing (at the very least) to them because of their (mis)understanding of what autism actually means. It's hardly surprising – after all, this book is littered with ableist examples from real life that we are living right now that will give credibility to internalized ableism.

Language

Language matters enormously. The way in which everyday parlance pervades the subconscious will almost invariably influence how one perceives any particular phenomena. For example, if you grow up in an environment in which a minority group (of any kind) is constantly belittled using pejorative language as a matter of course, then it is likely that this will influence your perspective over that minority group. This isn't to suggest that your attitude towards that group is wholly shaped by the daily narrative, but it is still very likely to play a fairly considerable role. Now take that example and extrapolate it to wider society; the language used around autism *as a matter of course* within society, as can be seen in the brief Google experiment earlier, is hugely problematic when it comes to attitudes and concepts of what being autistic means.

Examples of the sorts of ableist language prevalent today include:

- 'Symptoms'
- 'Condition'
- 'Impairments'
- 'Deficits'
- 'Disorder'
- 'Functioning – severity'.

I go further into functioning labels (including 'spectrum') in the next chapter. All the other terms are clearly negative in their connotations and application. I find it incredible that society is even *allowed* to refer to autistic human beings in this way. Sometimes, folk will suggest that rather than using 'disorder' as in Autistic Spectrum Disorder, it is preferable to use Autistic Spectrum Condition. I suppose that there is ever so slightly less ableist connotations but they are definitely still there. In the next chapter, you will find a suggested adjustment eradicating either terms.

Microaggressions

'Microaggressions' is a term that has been around for a while, but not specifically associated with the autism field. In terms of concept, I think it does fantastically well around identifying the problems with language. However, I am less convinced that the word itself does justice to the possible impact microaggressions actually have on autistic people in general.

Microaggressions are words or terms or assertions that are often subtle, often from an unconscious bias, but that marginalize and discriminate against an individual – and can be incredibly offensive. This is why I find the concept very useful – but the wording is not as powerful as perhaps it should be; and/or, perhaps too powerful at the same time.

Breaking 'microaggression' into two components leaves us with 'micro' and 'aggression'. As noted, the actual concept of the term is incredibly apt when applied to the autism field, but the components of the word itself may be misleading. 'Micro' suggests something minimal, small, possibly even trivial. This is not the case! I suspect that when the term was developed, it meant that the 'micro' aspect referred to intent coming from the 'perpetrator' rather than the impact on the receiver. Whatever the case, it must be noted very clearly that microaggressions against autistic people must be taken incredibly seriously – possibly 'macro' as a replacement would be more appropriate. Second, the 'aggression' part of the word denotes – at least to me – some level of consciousness and overt deliberate action. I don't think that people who could currently be accused of microaggressions fit this type. I know that there are some individuals who refer to autism very consciously and deliberately in a negative way, and autism as a word itself is sometimes to be found in popular culture as well as in society as a slur. However, in the main, microaggressions are usually found stemming from people out of ignorance rather than with malicious intent. This doesn't detract from their impact – but I am not sure that a culture of blame is the answer.

Many microaggressions come from a place of kindness, which, in a sense, makes it even worse. For example, there are just so many microaggressions that can occur at point of disclosure which can be hurtful enough to make a person no longer want to share. And having a barrier between you and sharing your authentic self is problematic indeed. So, for example, the three following examples are all possible microaggressions that, on the surface, appear to be born out of genuine kindness but have a semi-hidden rather dark message:

Are you sure your child is autistic, they are so good at [insert your own phrase]?

Essentially the well-meaning component is that the person delivering the response is identifying that your child is good at something. The microaggression, though, is the insinuation that being autistic means that you *can't* be good at it.

Oh dear, is there anything that can be done to help?

I guess that this one speaks for itself; the 'oh dear' could be seen as empathic, as could the query about wanting to help. However, the unstated implication is first sorrow that your child is autistic, second that being autistic suggests that they 'need help'.

That surprises me. You and your family are all so lovely ...

I know I've written about this elsewhere but I can't help myself because it's such a stark microaggression that helps make an important point. The response to disclosing that a parent and all their children are autistic identifies that the individual is surprised that there can even be a link between being autistic and being lovely. On the one hand the person is being kind by noting that the family are lovely – but the microaggression comes from the fact that there is a surprise that a child or adult can be both lovely *and* autistic.

Society is absolutely rife with microaggressions, and the impact is almost invariably negative. Being exposed to an ongoing barrage of microaggression is purely negative, and potentially devastatingly harmful. This area of ableism needs urgent attention; so:

Schools should add autism and other neurodivergences to the curriculum alongside more common topics of teaching around minority groups such as race and gender

Imagine a world in which, within education, it is just as common to have an assembly whereby the focus for the day is around the contribution that autistic people have had on the world, or how harmful autistic stereotypes are (not the fact that these stereotypes occur in the first place, but that they are so commonplace no one is really surprised). Developing a culture in education in which these areas are openly discussed in an accurate and informative way could go a long way towards reducing harmful impacts due to misinformation and misunderstandings.

Practice

The concept of microaggressions can seep into practice – what people want (or don't want) from the autistic child – and can be just as damaging as verbal microaggressions. The insinuation – or, in many cases, a clear assertion – that being one's authentic self is 'wrong' in some way can be soul-destroying. This book is all about reasonable adjustments, so I must keep this relatively brief (I also write in a similar vein in the later chapter concerning 'interventions'), but for the moment here are just a few examples of practice that could be considered as microaggressions.

Changing behaviour (e.g. preventing stimming)

There is so much literature that refers to 'autistic behaviour', and this always worries me to a certain degree. After all, what does it even mean? If one is autistic, then all of one's behaviour is 'autistic' in a way – and what we do know is that there is no behaviour that is exclusive to autistic people nor common to all autistic people. Taking those facts – and they *are* facts – into account, does the term 'autistic behaviour' convey much meaning? However, what is the case is that many behaviours that society associate with autism are often seen as negative and, subsequently, attempts might be made to suppress them. One obvious example of this is stimming – behaviour often displayed by individuals such as rhythmical movements, usually (but not always) used to self-regulate in some way. If an autistic child enjoys a stim – and let's face it, lots of autistic children genuinely love a good stim – then there should be time and (safe) space allocated to encourage it. I would go as far as to suggest that stimming should become a perfectly usual daily activity across society so that it no longer holds the prejudice that it often currently does. The suppression of a child's stimming – when that stimming comes from a place of positive energy – is not only a clear microaggression but also an impingement of their liberty and right to be themselves.

Making anyone feel bad for being autistic

This is a more general microaggression and can take a multitude of different forms.

> *Evan was out with his family on a day trip; he loves going out with his family but it also raises his anxiety somewhat as the day is far less predictable than his usual routine.*

43

However, he is keen to make the most of it and, being the kind of child who understands his anxiety very well, he makes sure that he balances out his instability by creating additional soothing 'stabilities' – for example, in the form of counting out loud the number of steps he takes in sequences of nine. He is aware that this isn't something that many people do and he doesn't want to draw unwanted attention to his family as he knows that they are sometimes embarrassed by his way of being, so he counts as quietly as possible. Even so, periodically throughout the day, his parents make mention of his counting, asking 'do you really have to do that?'

Even seemingly innocuous comments such as 'do you really have to do that?' when it is a natural and often necessary aspect of autistic life can make the child feel bad about themselves and their own authenticity. As is so common throughout the examples in this book, that single isolated 'incident' might appear fairly minor in and of itself. But that should not detract from the importance of recognizing it for what it is – a cog in the wheel of a major problem that can ruin the autistic life. While the parents are not deliberately asking the question to cause any distress, the message that Evan is getting is that his way of being is 'wrong'. Taken in combination with all the other ways in which autistic children can be made to feel inferior, this incident can be seen as an example of the real issue that needs addressing.

Shaming or excluding

Another example of ableist microaggression is when children are made to feel ashamed in some way for being who they are, sometimes in the form of being excluded. This is often seen within education when autism is almost used as an excuse to exclude a child. I know of far too many parents who have been asked to keep their child at home when the rest of the year group are going on a school trip, for example. Sometimes there may be a reason for this – but often it is simply very poor practice that sends a very negative message to the autistic child.

Making assumptions

Hannah is absolutely distraught but feels that she can't speak up at school because she feels too ashamed about the whole thing. She loves Christmas and all things related to it and has been looking forward to the school play for months. However, when it comes to choosing roles for who is going to play whom, the teacher in charge – a very kind person who really loves his role and wants what is best for his students – overlooks Hannah and doesn't even engage with her about the possibility of acting. Instead, he takes her to one side and tells her that he is aware that being autistic means that she will have different needs and that acting will be 'too much' for her, so he has allocated her a different role around costume design.

The teacher is well-meaning, no doubt about that at all; however, he has made an assumption – without involving Hannah – about what being autistic means; he's excluded her (albeit with good intentions) and has made her feel ashamed to be autistic.

Microaggressions and the concept of them form a hugely important component of many of the adjustments you will see running throughout this book. The idea that, *in isolation*, a word, phrase, idea, judgement (and so on) is essentially 'only' micro in and of itself and therefore does not require attention goes against the ethos of equality in my view. The very fact that these things *do not* occur in isolation is the whole point. It is the ongoing, consistent and perpetual nature of aggressions that can cause untold damage, which is why adjustments need to be made. So, as an example:

I think if I'd heard it once, then I'm not so sure I would have been that bothered. But hearing 'autism' being used as a slur – not every day but many days during the school term – was what caused me so much mental ill health in the long term. It was only when I discussed this during therapy that I even realized just how impactful it actually was. I never realized that my so very vulnerable child self was being 'told' that I was so awful that other kids used my way of being to belittle, tease and bully others. Comments such as 'you really are so autistic, no wonder you can't do ... ', or 'no wonder no one likes you, you're probably autistic or something' – these were the soundtrack to my time in the playground. They were never aimed at me – ironically enough the kids had such a misplaced view of autism that they never realized that I was (am) autistic, but hearing it vicariously directed at others in such a demeaning way meant that I subconsciously took it on board to apply to myself. I ended up as a teen having so much angst, hating the fact that I was autistic, always trying to be someone that I wasn't, always trying to be the least 'me' I possibly could, because the alternative would be that I thought no one could ever possibly like me, want to be with me, love me. Hating myself continued into my adult life, the depression, the cycle of doom of trying inordinately hard to be anyone other than me and failing miserably, only to beat myself up and do it all over again. The turning point came so many years later when I finally accepted my autistic self and discovered that those kids were wrong. It is not a slur – at least it should not be. It's ok. It's me, it's who I am and I've finally learned to at least start to like myself. But nothing will ever give me those years of anguish and torment back.

The fundamental truth (as I see it) is that exposure to negative aggressions can – and does – place individuals at a substantial disadvantage and is discriminatory. Therefore, treating them as *collectives* rather than isolated incidents is perfectly just and – dare I say it – reasonable.

Misinformation

How glorious would it be if the following suggestion was made into legislation:

All misinformation about autism is valid checked by an autistic-led authoritative body

In today's society of misinformation and with the lack of or verification of stories on social media, it is absolutely apt to point out that misinformation about autism has been rife ever since autism came into 'being' in academic terms, or even clinical terms. Obviously, autism has been around forever, so far as we can tell, but without an autism narrative we will not have understood it. Since the 1940s, autism has become more and more 'mainstream', to the point that almost all adults in current society would have heard of autism. Problematically, so many of those adults will also have a view as to 'what autism is'. I'm not sure that *anyone* can really 'know' 'what autism is' *relative to autistic people*, as being autistic will lead to different experiences and beings for each of those in the autistic population.

Some common myths that should always be challenged are included here (with explanations). I've deliberately written from an individual perspective and it is the same 'voice' throughout – this is deliberately playful, because it would be mythical in itself (or would it?) if all of those myths were associated with the same child. However, I have done this on purpose just to make the point around how incredibly frustrating, not to mention harmful, misinformation/ misconceptions can be.

Savantism

Everyone who meets my child has a different reaction when it comes to finding out that they are autistic. One of the most frustrating things is when a person bleats on and on about how they have seen some TV program about some guy or girl who was just amazing at whatever. I don't really care what it is that they were amazing at – common ones are musicians who are genius at playing the piano when they've never been taught how, or painters with amazing recall. My point is my child is not amazing at anything in particular, and the sense that I get when people tell me these stories – which, by the way, happens immediately on hearing that they are autistic – is that they expect me to then either identify with the story, as in 'yeah, he's good at the violin too, let me show you this' or come up with a different amazing talent. The fact that my child doesn't have one makes me oscillate between worrying that they don't actually believe my child is really autistic, and feeling a sense of disappointment from them that my child doesn't have anything 'special' to offer.

Being good at [maths/IT/computers/dinosaurs]

Ok, so once I've made my second disclosure – that my child is not to be compared to those lucky savants who certainly do exist but are very much in the minority, and certainly shouldn't be associated automatically with being autistic – all too often the conversation comes around to how autistic people might not be amazing at (whatever) but surely my child must have some kind of specialism – perhaps they're good with computers, or maths, or maybe they can fix an IT problem, or cite how many different types of dinosaurs ever existed. Why should they be associated with these subject areas? What is it about society that makes the leap that autism = maths (or whatever)? I don't want to get cancelled so I'd best be careful with what I say, but just imagine disclosing that you were of a particular ethnic minority and the immediate supposition was that you shared a key characteristic with the most famous person who shares that ethnicity? I mean, it just doesn't bear thinking about. And yet I have to put up with that kind of assumption from so many people when I tell them my child is autistic.

Being an adult
Such a weird one – and to be fair, it's becoming less common. But when I first went for my initial doctor's appointment, I was met with some level of confusion and was actually told that autism really only affected children. Even now I get asked things like 'oh, sure, but are you less autistic than when you were at school?' and similar sorts of questions. I find it extraordinary, really. I mean there aren't many facts that we can all confidently agree on about autism, but the fact that there's no cure, and that you're born autistic and therefore will die autistic is something that is clear for all to see. And yet I still get questioned about being an authentic autistic adult. Strange.

Being a girl
My child is definitely a boy. When it comes to me making a joke along the lines of 'well, it does run in the family – his sister is also autistic' and the response I get is 'oh, right – isn't that incredibly rare, for a girl to be autistic?' It drives me to distraction. In this day and age, with all the readily available information about how one can equally happily be an autistic girl as an autistic boy, let's get rid of the notion once and for all that autistic girls are rare!

Not being empathic

Interestingly, the conversations about empathy don't seem to focus on my son, they tend to focus on my daughter. Which is pretty ironic, seeing as she is extensively empathic. But I often get asked about her, 'does that mean she can't empathize?' or similar. It is literally one of the most common comments I hear about autism, and one which I get bored of having to refute. I genuinely worry about a society that associated autism almost automatically with empathy and lack thereof. I try not to think too much about it, but I do wonder at the level of damage that has been done to so many autistic individuals over the years when exposed to this kind of belief.

Not being excellent within a team

Ok – I fully understand that lots of autistic friends of mine tell me that they hate teamwork. I've done my own analysis, and it seems to me that every single one of them plays an incredibly important part of being within a group, but they still don't see themselves as team players. I keep telling them, 'not joining in with social aspects of the group doesn't devalue your importance of being part of that group' – sadly, society seems to dictate that we all need to be part of all aspects at all times in a group to hold the mantle of 'being a good team player'.

Being artistic – or, not being artistic!

Similar to a point I've already made, but this one really does frustrate me as it's a lose–lose situation. Folk seem to expect that my child is either really good at drawing from memory – or deny them the ability to be imaginative in an artistic, creative way! I mean, come on – not all of us are great artists, but nor do we lack creativity in the arts – far from it, trust me.

Brilliant at seeing detail

Yes, I've read the books, seen the films, heard the TED talks – but stop assuming that all autistic people are all the same and that they are all able to see detail in everything. I found this especially frustrating as my child does, in fact, see certain things in incredible detail – just not everything. One of their perhaps odder 'talents' is that they are quite easily able to see detail in tangles of things and are subsequently very good at untangling them. Shame there's no career in it, really. They love spending time untangling seemingly impossible jumbles of necklaces from an old jewellery box ...

Can't make eye contact

Yet another myth – either that my child can't make eye contact at all, that they are making eye contact (when they are not), or that fleeting eye contact means that they are 'not allowed' to be autistic. As far as myths about autism go, this really does cause problems – not least for those who are denied an autism identification because someone believes that autistic people can't have eye contact, and also, that the clinician thinks that they've witnessed eye contact when in reality they haven't.

Don't have imaginative play

I honestly thought that I didn't have imaginary play, because that is what the doctor told my Mum when he was assessing me. He'd come to school to watch me during the breaktime and because I was on my own doing apparently nothing much he concluded that I didn't play. Little did he know the amazing scenarios I was imaginatively creating about why so and so was talking to some one, and why such and such was happening. Getting utterly absorbed in my imagination, based on what I was watching, was both pure joy and a brilliant way to pass the time on my own –

a genuine comfort to me at the time. It was only when I was an adult recounting this that I was told that I realized that the doctor had been wrong, and that I was a highly imaginative and playful child – just not in the way that the doctor expected.

I was told that my daughter lacked imaginative play – it's all too easy to listen to the professional and believe what they say, but it never really sat well with me. I agree that her play was quite different from that of other kids her age, but that didn't detract from the fact that she demonstrated incredible imagination. Watching her develop intricate scenarios with her toys, chatting to them, giving them life, getting utterly absorbed in her creations – that seemed to me to be the opposite to what I was being told. When she got older, she would recount the times she spent engaged in this kind of activity – and I was right: she was using her imagination to an extraordinary degree. Just because it showed in a different way did not mean that she lacked imagination. She now uses her creativity in her vocational life!

Is related to intellect

It's never been directed at my child, but that doesn't make it any less problematic. Hearing assumptions that autistic people are either clever in some ways or have additional intellectual difficulties makes me wonder about its validity. So, far as I know, we don't actually know in any given population who is genuinely autistic – so how can there ever be any accurate statistics about what levels of intelligence autistic people are? For what it's worth, I suspect that autism is represented by people of all intellectual abilities.

Is caused by [vaccines/bad parenting/anything, really]

Aside from the genetic links that, in many families, are pretty obvious, will we ever find any definitive 'cause' of autism – as opposed to autism being a natural variant in human development? What we absolutely do know is that at the moment we cannot seriously say autism is caused by anything. We simply don't know. The notion that being a bad parent causes autism is, you might argue, so outdated that we can laugh about it. Why, then, are so many parents asked to go on a parenting course either prior to or following an autism identification?

Summation and nod to epistemic injustice

Epistemic injustice relates to injustices as a result of knowledge – or, at least, perceived knowledge. I will come back to the different types of epistemic injustice in later chapters, but it is worth mentioning it here because having a society that bases autism concepts on a model that does not align to the lived experiences of autistic people will heavily influence the levels of injustice that the autistic population will face. In relation to reasonable adjustments at a conceptual level, rather than a legal one, my argument is as follows: if it can be demonstrated that the autistic population are at risk of being at a substantial disadvantage as a result of misplaced conceptualizations of autism, then a reasonable adjustment might be that we – as a society – make every effort to combat those damaging notions in order to reduce risk of discrimination. Unfortunately, the Equality Act cannot be applied to society as a whole, but this should not detract from the principle that discourse, narrative, concepts and understanding play a crucial role in whether or not autistic individuals are at risk of epistemic injustice throughout all walks of life. What we can do, within the Equality Act, is identify organizations and institutions that promote narratives that could be deemed as increasing the risk of discrimination through ableist attitudes and encourage those attitudes to change.

3

Identification

- 'Diagnosis' is replaced by a more neutral term such as 'identification' while retaining the same clinical significance
- In all narratives, the term 'Autistic Spectrum Disorder' is replaced, simply, with 'autism'
- All neurodivergences are collated in a manual with the same clinical significance but without pejorative language or concepts
- Within a neurodivergence compendium, definitions and criteria are always written in neutral and/or affirmative language
- Autism waiting lists for assessment are eradicated and all identification processes take place within a month of original referral
- No child is refused an autism-identification process based on their intellectual ability
- Autism identification is a right, not something that needs fighting for
- Professionals show a willingness to listen to parents
- Autistic children have the right to have autism-qualified professionals undertaking assessments
- There are alternative assessments to in-clinic assessments
- Stop multiple clinicians asking the same questions

- Assessments not to be based on behaviour (or excluded based on behaviour) rather than cognitive processing
- Autism is not regarded as a 'trendy' label, nor seen as an 'excuse'

The wording in relation to autism identification is littered with ableist language and concepts that simply must change if society wants to stop exposing autistic children to the risk of feelings of inadequacies. Even before getting onto the terminology within the criteria, I suggest that adjustments can be made – first with the word 'diagnosis' and then second and third respectively with the words 'spectrum' and 'disorder'.

Google's English dictionary (provided by Oxford Languages) defines diagnosis as 'the identification of the nature of an illness or other problem by examination of the symptoms' as its primary definition. Autism is categorically not an illness. Nor would I regard autism as being a problem. The secondary definition is slightly less hideous but still problematic: 'the distinctive characterization in precise terms of a genus, species, or phenomenon'. Well, being autistic does not mean that one comes under the umbrella term of 'genus', and nor does it mean your child is of a different species! One could refer to autism as a phenomenon but it does seem somewhat impersonal at the very least.

Merriam-Webster's dictionary refers to diagnosis thus: 'the art or act of identifying a disease from its signs and symptoms' – autism is not a disease. The dictionary's secondary definition states that diagnosis is an 'investigation or analysis of the cause or nature of a condition, situation, or problem'. I don't subscribe to the notion that autism is a condition – nor is it a situation or problem.

Would it be reasonable to cease referring to autism as something that requires a diagnosis – as opposed, for example, to being identified, discovered or realized? As noted previously, language matters. Not only the terms themselves, but the connotations that are subconsciously reflected in the terms. Many people will associate the word 'diagnosis' – as very ably demonstrated by the dictionary definitions above – with something negative (such as an illness) that requires attention in terms of fixing or curing. While the term diagnosis itself won't automatically mean that the parent of a child will inexorably step on to the pathway of negativity and always see their child as a problem that requires fixing, there is, at the very least, a risk that the narrative infers – quite strongly – that being autistic *is* something problematic. And if, at the very start of their autism-discovery journey, the parent is being influenced by such ableist views, then the call for a reasonable adjustment becomes a just one. Therefore, I suggest:

'Diagnosis' is replaced by a more neutral term such as 'identification' while retaining the same clinical significance

The latter point is an important one. Some might argue that without a 'diagnosis', being autistic 'doesn't count' – so there needs to be the same credibility if the terminology changes. Having noted that, I don't think that I could suggest the following as a reasonable adjustment as such – but I am going to include it anyway as something to aspire to.

For a long time, autism has been associated with the term 'spectrum', and when used to denote the essential individuality of each autistic person, this is fine. My understanding is that the original use of the word 'spectrum' was, indeed, to refer to the vast range of individuals who are autistic. However, sometimes the word is used to infer that there is a range of 'autisms' that differ and can somehow be graded from mild to severe. As I've written elsewhere (e.g. Chapter 2 of *Autism in Adults*, Chapter 3 of *Autism in Children*, Chapter 3 of *Avoiding Anxiety in Autistic Children*, Chapter 2 of *Avoiding Anxiety in Autistic Adults*, Chapter 2 of *What Works for Autistic Children*), I absolutely reject this notion as I find it eminently harmful and disrespectful – which is why I feel that the word 'spectrum' should play no part in the identification process. Along with 'spectrum' comes the word 'disorder'. The actual term in both DSM-5 and ICD-11 is 'Autistic Spectrum Disorder' – in other words one is not even *allowed* at a clinical level to 'be autistic', one has to be diagnosed (identified) as 'having an Autistic Spectrum Disorder'. Quite why we still have such ableist language at the very heart of the identification amazes me; straight away, it positions your child as disordered – and this is before a critique of the actual criteria itself. A suggested amendment (and, therefore, adjustment) is that:

In all narratives, the term 'Autistic Spectrum Disorder' is replaced, simply, with 'autism'

Doing this might cost something in terms of reprints, for example of paper-based school policies; however, in the main it costs *absolutely nothing* in terms of financial costs. It takes a little bit of effort (though let's be fair, not much) – but what it does cost is a level of consistent agreement and motivation. However – my argument is that consistency and motivation should be reasonable adjustments themselves (see more on consistency below). My rationale for why we need to be motivated to make this seemingly minor change is the disparity between 'minor' and 'significance'. Of course, it is minor making a change to a phrase (or, in this case, turning a phrase into a single word) but the significance is potentially huge. Changing societal perception of autism from something negative and 'disordered' to something far more neutral (and, in my view, accurate) can not only lead to a significant shift change in attitude towards autistic people but also decrease risk of internalized ableism for that specific population.

Where does autism fit?

Continuing from some of the concepts in the previous chapters, until society adjusts its understanding of autism there will be risks of ableism and disadvantages. The fact that autism is defined within two medical-based manuals is, therefore, troubling in and of itself. The DSM-5 (currently) and ICD-11 (currently) are the latest manuals to include autism criteria. The criteria itself is problematic enough, which I will come on to discuss – but what about the fact that autism is situated in those manuals in the first instance?

Both of these manuals are meant for clinicians – clinicians who, in the main, are medically trained and taught about autism from a medical-model deficit-based paradigm. The catch-22 here is obvious to see. If clinicians are led by their training and that training is based on medical-model manuals with the deficit-based criteria, then those clinicians are more likely to understand autism within the 'disordered' category. This becomes cyclical if that 'knowledge' is then passed on to autistic children during the assessment process and, at the same time, to parents. What chance do clinicians have if the 'standard' manuals are so medical-model based that clinicians *have* to abide by a medical-model set of criteria in order to identify autism? In a sense, their hands are tied right from the outset. I was challenged recently about this – which provides a great example of the problem. A group of very forward-thinking clinicians were asking about report writing. Their point was that in order to fulfil the 'diagnostic criteria', their reports *had* to situate autism as a set of deficits, otherwise, ironically, the child would not meet that criteria. But they also recognized that this neither gave a full picture of the child's profile, nor did it allow for a more neutral or even positive representation of the autistic profile.

One possible solution might be:

All neurodivergences are collated in a manual with the same clinical significance but without pejorative language or concepts

I adore this suggestion. I also feel that such a compendium should be neurodivergence-led and 'approved' by the neurodivergent community as much as this is possible. I critiqued DSM-5 in the book *What Works for Autistic Adults* and essentially demonstrated how criteria is considered in a different way to mean the same or a very similar thing but without the necessity of making it an impairment-based set of criteria. Therefore, another suggestion:

Within a neurodivergence compendium, definitions and criteria are always written in neutral and/or affirmative language

This may sound easier said than done, but it is certainly something to aspire to. After all, if we are understanding autism through the lens of current definitions, then who knows what damage is being done.

In addition to the simple task of changing society's view of autism forever with a brand-new neurodivergence compendium that should be lauded and recognized worldwide, we need to pay attention to some other aspects of autism identification to ensure that children are not discriminated against.

Waiting lists

I genuinely believe that waiting lists discriminate against autistic children. They can do so in a minimum of three ways:

1 Parental understanding
2 Understanding of self
3 School's understanding.

Parental understanding

We used to bemoan the fact that we had such a naughty child and, to be honest, we used to have so many discussions about where we were going wrong. We are good people, we're good parents – he's got an older sibling who fits the profile of a perfect daughter, so we must be doing something right. Just what was it, we used to say to one another, that made our son so impolite, so snappy, so full of rage and anger? What was it that made him not listen to us, or even listen to us and then ignore us? It was infuriating. We never said it to one another, but secretly, in our darkest moments, I for one used to wonder what we had done to even deserve such a child. In hindsight, I shudder at what we used to talk about and what I used to think. How little did I know. Whoever said 'ignorance is bliss' was certainly not applying the concept to how we understood our gorgeous, loveable, loving boy.

What a change his autism identification made. What a difference when we leaped into the autism world, following autistic bloggers, watching autistic vloggers, reading autistic autobiographies, listening to autistic speakers and generally engaging with the autistic community. What we learned from them and were able to apply to our amazing son changed our family forever – not least our relationship with our son, but also his relationship with his sister and with himself. Here are just a few examples stemming from the above:

We thought he was impolite – rubbish! At times he was blunt to the point of us thinking he was impolite.

Now we just know he is a far more honest child compared to others, and has an incredible way of noticing and pointing things out that others might not even notice. Ok, so sometimes that means we are told that our hair smells bad, or the car isn't as clean as next door's, or that our grammar is spectacularly awful – but these things are, after all, absolutely true. We also wondered why he ignored us – he didn't; we just weren't being clear with what we wanted him to do. Simply saying 'wouldn't it be just amazing if you tidied your room?' has nothing to relate to our son; he doesn't think it would be amazing, and it's not an instruction anyway, so it's perfectly safe to ignore. Snappy? Full of rage? Full of anger? Relooking at those horrific judgements we made through his autism lens, and realizing that we were guilty of exposing him to so much anxiety, so much of the time – we soon realized that, in reality, he was far less 'snappy' or 'angry' than he had a right to be. In fact, we now understand that he is an incredibly gentle child who used to hate the way he reacted – he just had very little choice or control over himself. Imagine being so distressed on a day-to-day basis that you lose control? And him being just a kid? We really wish we'd known his autism truth far, far sooner.

Understanding of self

Before I knew about autism, I used to just think I was useless. It was annoying, as I was reasonably sure that I shouldn't be useless because I'm a fairly intelligent kid, so I would try so hard to be as good as everyone else at what I now know to be very autism-unfriendly activities – at least very autism-unfriendly from my perspective. Now that I know I'm autistic, I don't blame myself anymore, nor do I force myself to be someone that I will never be. Instead, I put all my energy into being the best autistic version of myself that I can be –

and it works a treat. It's just a shame that I had to waste all that time lying awake at night thinking I was useless, and wondering what I could do about it.

School's understanding

It was the most eye-opening process I had ever gone through as a teacher. I had no idea at all that she was autistic – mostly because I didn't realize it at the time, but also because my understanding of autism was so awful. Now, I am blown away at the difference it has made, not only to the school but more importantly to her wellbeing and subsequent education. We used to operate in such a culture of blame – blame the child for her behaviour, blame the parents for not being able to sort out their daughter and, I'm sad to say, that even when she got her diagnosis, there were some staff who blamed the autism – 'well, she is just like that because she's autistic', I heard someone say. Now we have changed our minds considerably, and I am left wondering why, as a teacher, I had such a shocking understanding of how an autistic student experiences life. The distress that I personally must have caused her, the sensory agony of the classroom, the sheer overwhelm that she used to have to endure on a day-to-day basis. I am so aware that we can never get those years back for her – what a wasted opportunity missed, what a miscarriage of justice that she had to wait for such a long time for us all to find out just who she was.

Would it be too much to ask for there to be a recognition that waiting lists can, in fact, put children at a substantial disadvantage, and that:

Autism waiting lists for assessment are eradicated and all identification processes take place within a month of original referral

There are clearly resource implications for achieving this, but logically the actual duration of assessment is not dependent on waiting lists. In other words, however long or short the waiting list, the assessment itself will take however long it takes. This means that getting rid of waiting lists in one fell swoop should mean, assuming numbers of children being referred doesn't change over time, they can be gotten rid of forever. Spending money for this is a one-off and, given that the impact will influence the waiting time for *every single child* thereafter, and the impact could be seen as substantial (in a positive way), one might begin to understand that *not* getting rid of waiting lists could be seen as discriminatory.

Getting an autism identification

My next suggested adjustment is a really easy one, and I've only included it because of the various reports from parents that I have heard over the years:

No child is refused an autism-identification process based on their intellectual ability

This has (not) worked both ways; in other words, I have heard that parents of children with learning disabilities have been told 'it's not worth having an autism assessment', and equally I've heard that 'she can't be autistic because she's too intelligent'. Intelligence has nothing whatsoever to do with whether one is autistic – you can be autistic and be of any intellect. This brings me on to another seemingly simple one, but which is perhaps less easy to translate into practice:

Autism identification is a right, not something that needs fighting for

Far too many children are being let down by being denied the opportunity to find out about themselves through the identification process. Being 'rejected' by gatekeepers should not be an option. I've always been an advocate of removing as many barriers to the identification as possible, so including direct self-referrals should be as standard. The arguments that so many parents will subsequently want an autism assessment seem ludicrous. Why would parents seek an autism assessment if there wasn't any indication that their child was autistic? Yes, there might be a very small population of people who go down this route, just as there are in all walks of life, but this shouldn't mean that the majority need to suffer as a result. If autism identification were an option for all, then over time there would be a far more accurate reflection of who autistic children were. The benefits of this include:

Better understanding of who the autistic children actually are

We currently don't know who the autistic children are. Comparing estimated prevalence rates with incidence numbers, there is almost always (if not always) a clear disparity between the two. If prevalence rates are the actual number of autistic children within a given population *with a diagnosis*, and the incidence rates are the *actual number of autistic children irrespective of whether they have been identified*, then the commonality is that prevalence rates are lower – often significantly – than incidence rates. Therefore, there are plenty of autistic children who remain unidentified. If we believe that supporting autistic children appropriately starts with knowing who they are in the first place, then better identification systems and reduction of barriers to those systems can only be a good thing.

Better understanding of the type and scale of services that are required

If we don't know who the population consists of, then it is extremely difficult to know what support they are likely to need. Even more difficult is the knowledge of what sort of scale that support should look like.

Better chance of positive autistic wellbeing across the age range

The outcomes of clarity over who is autistic, followed by appropriate measures to ensure that their needs are met, should mean that there is an increased chance of autistic wellbeing throughout childhood and beyond. Without knowing who those children are, it is reasonable to suggest that there is an increased risk of not supporting them in the right way.

Reduction in overall resources to society

All of the above might sound horrific to those holding the purse strings. But let's break it down with a few key points:

1 Autistic children may well cost more if left unidentified.
2 Short-term increases in costs may very well lead to a decrease in costs overall.
3 Non-identified autistic children may be more expensive for less gain in other areas of society.

Autistic children may well cost more if left unidentified

Without an identification and autism-friendly support, some children could end up increasingly costing Local Authorities in other ways. For example, children excluded from schools ending up in high-cost specialist settings when this could have been avoided is one very clear example of how things might have differed had the individual received more appropriate, autism-specific support originally.

Short-term increases in costs may very well lead to a decrease in costs overall

Poorly supported autistic children, for many of the reasons identified in this book, will be at a greater risk of having all sorts of problems that can filter into adulthood. The stark statistics around autism and, for example, employment (lack of) notwithstanding, the non-economic costs, such as personal cost to wellbeing, paint a very grim picture. It would seem perfectly sensible to suggest that creating happy autistic children with the right levels of support is more likely to subsequently lead to happy autistic adults.

Non-identified autistic children may be more expensive for less gain in other areas of society

This point relates to misidentification of other issues that are 'instead of' the autism identification. So, for example, a misdiagnosis of borderline personality disorder (BPD), with all the therapy and support that might be given, could well be a waste of time and resources if the reality for the young person is that they are autistic, and don't have BPD. Similarly, one is reminded of cases whereby a young person has been diagnosed as anorexic when in fact they are autistic with all sorts of sensory issues with food, and the 'treatment' options are both inappropriate and ineffective.

Expectations of professionals

Professionals show a willingness to listen to parents

As elsewhere, this sounds like a somewhat ludicrous suggestion to make. However, gather a group of parents under one roof and ask for a show of hands after asking the question 'have you always been listened to and felt that your voice was heard when engaging with professionals about your child?'

and see what happens. Not a very scientific claim, I know – but if you don't believe me, give it a go. How much wasted time, effort and money stem from parents not being believed when they first raise their thoughts about the possibility of their child being autistic? And yet how often are those very same parents eventually vindicated when it becomes apparent that they were right all along. Many parents become experts on their own children, and yet far too often they are not seen as such. This doesn't mean to say that all parents are always autism experts in reference to their children, but parents are often likely to have far greater knowledge about their child than a professional first encountering them, so giving parents a voice seems like a sensible adjustment to me.

Autistic children have the right to have autism-qualified professionals undertaking assessments

I am absolutely not wanting to suggest that professionals involved in autism identifications don't have expertise. However, there is no statutory obligation around what autism-specific background professionals need to have before being a part of that process. I find this extraordinary. Basically, a child can be assessed by someone who has had very limited input on autism as part of their clinical journey; despite this there is still an assumption that this limited input is of sufficient standard to understand how best to conduct themselves. I appreciate that there are all sorts of training courses – some of them specific to providing assessments, which is all well and good. However, it still remains that a clinical professional doesn't have to have autism-specific qualifications to conduct autism-specific assessments. I genuinely find this extraordinary. If we were to 'allow' general clinicians to avoid autism assessments, and all assessments were undertaken by autism-qualified clinicians who have taken an 'approved' autism assessment qualification (e.g. a post graduate award specific to autism and identification), then surely this would alleviate waiting lists and at the same time increase accuracy of autism assessment outcomes. Just imagine if every single person involved had to qualify with an award that included, for example, the following:

- How to engage with parents from day one
- What language is best to use
- An in-depth reflection of the pros and cons of autism theory
- How to reduce anxiety for all those involved in the process
- The purpose of the assessment process
- An in-depth understanding of the autistic constellation
- Myths of autism
- Autism and sensory issues
- How to write up assessment reports.

I'll stop there otherwise I am inclined to write an entire course content – but you get the gist. I for one am absolutely convinced that *reducing* the pressure on clinicians to provide autism assessments and *increasing* pressure on the necessity for having autism-specific clinicians would then *reduce* waiting lists and costs and massively *increase* the potential of autistic wellbeing across society.

There are alternative assessments to in-clinic assessments

We are well aware that many autistic children suffer from anxiety, and if there is anything that can be done to reduce that anxiety then it should be considered. I am aware that some provision requires parents to bring their child into a clinical setting – many of which attempt to be as child-friendly as possible. However, if we go back to the concept of reasonable adjustments, and ask the question whether taking a child to an unknown environment with no beneficial outcome (from the perspective of the child) places that child at risk of elevated anxiety, then would it be reasonable – if an alternative was readily available – to utilize that option? Plenty of professionals habitually organize home visits, for example, so why can't this be an option for a child for whom the alternative leads to acute anxiety? Taking this a step further, just in case this option is not taken seriously: we do know that children who suffer from anxiety overload – which then leads to major complications such as distressed behaviour or shutdown – are far more likely to have long-lasting negative implications compared to children who are anxiety-free. It goes back to the point earlier about microaggressions. It is the ongoing nature of anxiety that can lead to very real issues. Therefore, we should be taking very measured steps to do what we can to eliminate anxiety when it is reasonable to do so.

Stop multiple clinicians asking the same questions

A very simple one, but something that so many parents find incredibly frustrating – the necessity for them to have to answer the same questions multiple times simply because they are being asked by different professionals. Surely it is not too much to ask for there to be a consensus among professionals over what information is to be collated by whom? Of course, there will be some overlap, but the principle remains the same.

Assessments not to be based on behaviour (or excluded based on behaviour) rather than cognitive processing

I will reiterate – I am not a clinician, so in many ways many people will come up with many reasons as to why I shouldn't be commenting on these sorts of issues. My perspective comes from engaging with the autism world both academically and in real life; and my understanding, absolutely categorically, is that there is no behaviour that is specific solely to autistic children. I've written about this elsewhere. This adjustment is more along the lines – and this is based on real-life examples – of where a child has been denied an autism identification because the clinician is insisting that they are either looking for something specific that is 'missing' (e.g. repetitive behaviours) or they have witnessed a behaviour that they believe excludes autism (e.g. imaginative play).

Autism is not regarded as a 'trendy' label, nor seen as an 'excuse'

This is yet another cultural one, but it would be so refreshing for parents to not have to navigate attitudes such as autism being viewed as the 'latest trend' or as 'an excuse' for their child being who they are. Autism is not 'trendy' nor is it an excuse – and nor, by the way, is it a label in the way that people sometimes refer to it as:

Are you sure you want to go down that route? After all, autism is just a label, it won't make any difference …

Yes, I am sure. If you are interested in labels, then here is a list for you:

- *Naughty*
- *Uncompliant*
- *Defiant*
- *Odd*
- *Weird*
- *Rude*
- *Malicious*
- *Anti-social*
- *Challenging.*

I could go on. But I won't because it's too distressing for me to think of all the horrific labels that have unfairly been applied to my autistic child. Autism is not a label, it's a truth.

4

School

- There is an adequate range of educational options available for all autistic children
- All schools have a statutory duty to provide autistic-led training as a minimum for half a day each term
- For the SENCO in all schools to have an appropriate Post Graduate Autism qualification
- Autism leads in schools engage in peer-support sessions within their region
- All staff take it in turns for a few days a year to be seconded into some kind of setting that supports adults
- Reward systems are either removed or very carefully considered
- All school policies are reviewed and updated by a panel of expert autistic educators
- Ensure that homework is set with no ambiguity and appropriate guidance
- Provide alternatives to doing homework at home
- Whenever an examination is not required, it is replaced with a more suitable mode of knowledge transfer
- All exam questions are reviewed by a panel of autistic adults to ensure that they are fit for purpose
- Questions can be asked in a variety of different formats and at different times
- All teaching comes in different formats
- Headphones are a common feature in the classroom

- Focus equipment is not only allowed but encouraged
- Seating is allocated based on the needs of the student
- Certain subjects are taught with elements of autism-specificity as and when required
- As well as more standard sex and relationships education within Personal, Social, Health and Economic (PSHE) lessons, additional information pertinent to autistic students is covered within appropriate groups
- Students have far greater say in which subjects they choose to study
- Students can study subjects in blocks
- There is an autodidactic offer for those who prefer it
- Breaktimes include alternative options for safe spaces
- Lunch is offered in a variety of different spaces, including solitary spaces
- Eating with hands is a standard practice and food is offered in self-appointed receptacles
- Autistic eating requirements are taken just as seriously as other dietary ones
- All autistic students have their key primary needs identified and highlighted to all teaching staff on a daily basis

Where even to start? Well – let's start big. My suggested reasonable adjustment – 'simply' – is that:

There is an adequate range of educational options available for all autistic children

Not too much to ask, is it? Ok – so within the Equality Act, this might not appear at first glance to fit the description as regards resources, particularly financial. But I wonder if, on balance, there could be an argument for it. By range of resources, I would include properly funded education at home and flexi-schooling as genuine options. If budgets were shifted and allocated to the child and greater autonomy given to families regarding how best to fund education, then perhaps these options would not be as financially prohibitive as it might seem. Of course, there would need to be clear guidance and regulation, but as a system it might work. The reason why I feel that it is a necessity to dramatically change the way in which we educate our children is because so many of them are being failed. Exclusion rates for autistic children are high; so-called 'school refusers' are often, in reality, autistic children who have been traumatized by their school experience, and many adults report on just how influential a negative experience within education has been and the impact it has on them throughout adulthood. If a dramatic reframe of educational offer subsequently has a dramatic impact on whole generations of children, then I feel it is worth fighting for. However, for the time being, I will focus more on what can be changed in the interim while we are waiting for the entire education system to be rebooted.

In this chapter, I am well aware that I am often painting schools/staff in a negative manner. I am fully appreciative that many, many schools and many, many staff are exemplary and do a fantastic job under extremely trying circumstances – so I apologize in advance for the negative tone of the narrative.

While this whole book is dedicated to reducing risk of discrimination to autistic children, many of the examples of possible changes in practice – particularly in this chapter on education in school – will be of potential benefit to a much wider group of students. In general, one might go by the concept that improving practice to make it suitable for autistic children in general will likely improve practice for everyone.

What teachers need to know

It amazes me that autistic children are so often at the mercy of well-meaning teaching staff who have very little knowledge or understanding of autistic needs. It seems grossly unfair, both for the teaching staff and for the children – and the damage that can be done is unquestionable. Surely, even timely reminders that their autistic pupils have needs that might be different from those of their non-autistic peers would be a reasonable request as a mandatory baseline. So:

All schools have a statutory duty to provide autistic-led training as a minimum for half a day each term

I've included the term 'autistic-led' as there are so many amazing autistic speakers who are willing to share their experiences and feel that they are the ones often best placed to influence practice for the better. It should be noted here that training needs to take a whole-school approach; indeed, I believe that it should go even further. I am a huge fan of parents being included alongside school staff so that the same information is being shared. Parents should also have the opportunity to feed back on the training, especially if they feel that something has been raised that they disagree with. Far too often, parents are not seen as the experts in their own children, and involving them as part of the training processes in school could go some way towards alleviating that. In addition to parents, the whole-school approach should include staff who are not classed as educators but who still play an invaluable role in children's educational experience. This would include, for example, those who are involved at lunch times and those providing transport.

However, 'simple' training days are not enough if we really want to provide appropriate education within schools for autistic pupils. There also needs to be a level of autism-specificity for key staff, and the most appropriate role would be the allocated SENCO (Special educational needs coordinator). Therefore, an adjustment would be:

For the SENCO in all schools to have an appropriate Post Graduate Autism qualification

While there are cost and time implications for this, the level of expertise that is needed in schools goes beyond termly training sessions. It is not feasible, much as I'd like it, for all staff to have autism qualifications, but it is definitely feasible for there to be a requirement for at least one member of staff to lead on autism-related issues. Having an autism lead in every single school could make a huge difference in terms of practice. In order to ensure that these autism leads do not feel isolated, I would add another adjustment:

Autism leads in schools engage in peer-support sessions within their region

Having the opportunity to have time and space provided to meet up with other autism leads within a specified region to share practice and provide peer support could also have a dramatic impact on how autistic students are educated. It will help with consistent good practice, is easy to organize and costs very little, aside from time.

One final adjustment specific to staff before I move on:

All staff take it in turns for a few days a year to be seconded into some kind of setting that supports adults

The rationale for this is there is a need for staff working with children to have a constant reminder that the children they are supporting grow into adults, and that their educational experience *will* have an impact on their adult life. This sounds almost unbelievably ridiculous – of course staff are aware that the children they support grow into adults. But there is a difference between knowing something at a fundamental level and actually taking it into account in practice. Having the stark reminders of the impact (positive as well as negative) that education has for the longer-term future could be something that is highly impactful within educational provision.

I have written extensively about the reduction of anxiety in schools (*Avoiding Anxiety in Autistic Children*) as well as possible good practice (*What Works for Autistic Children*) but here are some possible reasonable adjustments for consideration in addition to those books.

Reward systems are either removed or very carefully considered

Some folk like the idea of rewards systems, but I know of plenty of autistic children who have been damaged by the implementation of reward systems such as visual reward charts. Imagine that you are the child who constantly doesn't meet the expectations and who has to go through the humiliation of everyone seeing that you have 'failed' – it is essentially public shaming for many children. And this doesn't even take into account what the reward system is actually for.

> *I feel so aggrieved with school about the way they treat my amazing child. How many times do I need to explain to them that their 'good behaviour' chart puts him at a massive disadvantage? In fact, I believe that it actively discriminates against him because they are judging him against what they believe to be good behaviour, without taking autism into account whatsoever. Movement is a necessity for him, not a choice, so punishing him for not sitting still – which, for some reason, they have judged to be a key component of 'good behaviour' – is simply unfair. And then they humiliate him every single day by identifying that his is the behaviour that requires*

attention on the chart. Basically, they are trying to mould him into someone he will never be – and what damage is being done in the meantime?

This brings me on to more specific school policies, which absolutely need attention to ensure that they do not discriminate against the child. The wording, for example, of a behaviour policy is critical to make sure that children are not being judged through the wrong lens. Notions of what constitutes 'good' behaviour, for example, will differ considerably depending on how good an understanding individual staff have of their autistic pupils. Therefore, all school policies must be worded so that they offer protection for different ways of being in school. This is not a request to make excuses – which is often a response I hear – it is a genuine need for autism to be considered at a policy level to avoid discrimination. One way forward that I feel would make a massive impact and reduce risk of discrimination would be the following adjustment:

All school policies are reviewed and updated by a panel of expert autistic educators

It is very possible that with this very simple adjustment being implemented, much of the potential for discriminatory practice would diminish. However, it would be remiss not to make special mention of three specific policies that are often the cause of problems for the autistic population, which are:

- Behaviour policies
- Inclusion policies
- Uniform policies.

Behaviour policies

One of the biggest challenges with behaviour policies is that of judgement: the judging of what constitutes 'good' behaviour in the first instance. Many policies will include wording such as 'reward good behaviour', 'no tolerance for poor behaviour', 'proper regard for authority' or – this is one that I came across recently – 'recognizes behaviour norms and positively reinforces this behaviour'. The issue, fairly obviously, is that so often the 'go to' benchmark for all of these is based on the PNT construction of what such behaviour might look like. Conversely, and possibly even more problematically, authentic autistic ways of being might be deemed as poor behaviour if individual needs are not taken into account. For example:

> In order to fulfil her sensory needs as well as keep her anxiety to a minimum, Jo needs to make sure that she does a number of things throughout the school day. These include, for example, using one specific toilet (she has an intense level of anxiety about using the toilet and only feels safe in the one at the end nearest the door), making sure that her desk is free from clutter at all times (which means she keeps much of her stationery on the floor by her feet), and making sure that she is the first person to leave the classroom at the end of every lesson. The culmination of these necessities is that Jo is often accused of time-wasting (waiting for the 'right' toilet to use even though there may be others vacant), being untidy and contravening the Health and Safety policy (due to her keeping equipment on the floor) and bullying (when she pushes past other students to make sure that she leaves the classroom first). She is often in trouble for 'breaking the rules' according to various school policies – and yet she is simply being her own authentic autistic self.

Inclusion policies

What inclusion means to one person might look vastly different to another. This is just one of the reasons why inclusion policies that are generic in nature can be so problematic at an individual level. Three key 'mistakes' that a school might make are:

Thinking that inclusion means integration

Inclusion is not synonymous with integration. Just being in the same space as everyone else is not the same as having one's needs met at an inclusive level.

> *For years I made sure that just before any break time, I did something that would warrant an indoor detention. The idea from a school perspective was that indoor detention was a punishment, being cooped up on your own inside while everyone else went out to play. The irony is that, for me, being on my own indoors was exactly what I wanted – the thought of integration with the other kids filled me with terror, so working out just the right kind of wrongdoing was an essential part of my school day. It was quite a tough ask, and I didn't always get it right, but it was also quite good fun while it lasted. Luckily, they never figured it out; unluckily, my poor parents were so often hauled in to get told off for my behaviour – it must have driven them mad.*

Believing that all pupils want the same thing in relation to inclusion

There is no 'one size fits all' approach to inclusion. What one autistic child finds inclusive may differ from another child. One of the perennial problems in school is the belief that doing really well with supporting a child in the past automatically means that utilizing similar approaches will work just as well in the future. They might help – but equally, they might not! Similarly, having a sense of feeling included, and heard, and respected for one child may come in a very different form of practice compared to someone else.

> *I simply have to be heard, I have to have a voice, I have to have a say in what is happening, what is going on around me. I like to be the one organizing others, I like to be the team captain, I like to be the decision maker. Without some level of control, I am lost, bereft, scared, anxious to the point of not being able to function. Even giving me simple roles like taking the register to the head office gives me a glorious sense of purpose. I adore being a go-to person – I know it can't be like that all of the time, but having some level of control at least some of the time and being recognized for that role is so important to me.*

> *I hate being in any kind of spotlight; I find any kind of attention drawn to me akin to bullying. Being left to my own devices, being the quiet one industriously getting on with things, going under the radar – that is what inclusion means to me. To be allowed to be anonymous – that is my safe haven, and feeling safe is what I crave over anything else.*

Choosing equality over equity

There is a marked difference between providing *equal* access to opportunities and providing the *same* access to them. If we understand equality to be synonymous with 'same', then the application of equality among a group of children with diverse and different needs will, by definition, advantage some over others.

> *I am just so fed up with school making out that it's ok to treat my child in the same way as everyone else. He is autistic, his needs are different from others. Treating him*

the same is to deny his right to be treated as an individual, with his own needs. It's pure discrimination and I simply don't buy into these comments that 'he needs to learn to do things the same as everyone else otherwise how will he get on in life?' Just the other day, he came home utterly distraught. Of course, he is way too sensitive to say anything at school so it only ever comes out when he is safe at home, then we really feel the brunt of it – and I can't blame him. He told me about how the class had been told to write a poem – sounds simple enough, I guess. The problem was that they had to share these poems with the kid next to them, and because my lad loves words and is so advanced for his age, he wanted to create a haiku – but was told he needed to make it simpler, otherwise others wouldn't understand it, and everyone else was doing a rhyming couplet. I don't get why he wasn't just allowed to do both, and share his haiku with the teacher instead of the chap sat next to him – such a simple solution to a problem that need never to have existed.

Buying into a philosophy of needs-led equity would make such a difference to so many pupils.

Uniform policies

Uniforms and uniform-related stories seem to crop up quite a bit in the news. The easiest concept to adhere to when it comes to making sure that autistic children are not discriminated against is simply to 'allow' as much choice as is humanly possible. I am not decrying the arguments about why schools need a uniform or a uniform policy – those debates are a separate issue – but I am suggesting that without wriggle room (pardon the pun) within the uniform policy, there is a risk of clear discrimination. I am reminded of the individuals who have shared with me their need to wear shorts instead of trousers, for example. They may be in the minority, but if a child *needs* to wear shorts and it is not covered within the school's policy, then they might be severely disadvantaged. From a sensory perspective alone, if the feeling of touch against the knees is processed as pain (which, for some autistic people, is the case), then forcing a child to wear trousers is the equivalent of sentencing them to ongoing pain on a daily basis while at school.

School rules

Almost all schools will have school rules. But they sometimes seem to lack the flexibility required to fully take autistic needs into account. And not taking autistic need into account leads to an increased likelihood of autistic pupils being at a disadvantage. Here are some examples of real school rules that I know of that have disadvantaged autistic children:

> **Rule: we walk in school; we never run**
> *And yet it appears to be utterly unacceptable for my child to send in a formal complaint about his teacher to the Head after noting that one particular teacher can frequently be witnessed running in between lessons. In fact, the Head remonstrated with my child for 'telling tales'. I'm not at all convinced that they understand just how traumatic the whole thing is for her; she is inconsolable. How can it be justifiable for a teacher, a person of responsibility, to flout the rules and then for her to get into trouble for reporting it? I'm also seriously concerned now that she will think that it's perfectly ok to break whatever rules she likes. Until now she has been super careful to abide by whatever rules that have been put in place, both at home and at school – I don't know what the future holds for her now.*

Rule: we look after our things; we don't break or lose them

Poor Fran is just so stressed, and this is after only her first ever day at school. They went through the rules and were really quite strict about it. No room for error, it seems. They made the class sit there while the Head went through each rule, and she was adamant that all children needed to stick to the rules as it was their school philosophy that everyone has to abide by the rules to make it a good environment to be in. The trouble is that Fran has major issues with her coordination; it's a sensory thing – and clumsy would be a polite way of describing her. We have always made light of it, ever since she started bumping into things as soon as she could move – it's almost become a bit of a family joke, and we have made sure she never feels bad about it. After all, it's definitely not her fault, it's just the way that she is made. Now she's super scared of going into school in case she breaks their rule. Surely, it's not ok for a child to be scared of going to school?

Rule: we are polite and always use kind language

George got into trouble – again. The issue is that what one person thinks is kind is not the same as what George thinks is kind. George is one of those no-nonsense children who is always on the lookout for other people; he genuinely has their wellbeing at heart. And yet school so often think he's being mean. The latest in the ongoing saga was when he (politely) told one of his schoolmates that she smelled terrible. His view, which he did explain to no avail, was that he didn't know if she was aware of just how terrible she smelled and so he thought he would point it out in case she wanted to do something about it. It came from a genuine place of kindness, which is ironic seeing as it was the 'kind rule' that he was subsequently accused of breaking.

Rule: we treat others the same as we would like to be treated

I don't know about anyone else, but whenever I try to treat those around me in the way that I want to be treated, it seems to backfire. I want to talk about the ethics of keeping animals in captivity along with issues such as the environment. I want to talk about these for as long as I am allowed, and whenever I get the chance. So that's what I do – I treat others to lots of very interesting information about zoos and global warming but then I get told off by the teacher for not chatting about anything else. I don't know; I follow the rules and still get into trouble.

Rule: put your hand up if you've got a question

How many times do I have to be told to lower my hand? It feels like it happens over and over. It's just not fair – the rule is to raise my hand when I've got a question, and I have just so many questions! But no one told me that apparently there are rules within rules and that I somehow have to guess which of my perfectly reasonable questions appear reasonable to the teacher. Otherwise, they get so fed up with me doing exactly as the rule asks that they just shut me down. I am so confused.

Rule: listen to your classmates when they are supposed to be speaking

And yet I get told off for doing exactly that! The rule should be more like 'listen to your classmates when they are supposed to be speaking and have been asked to speak by the teacher; otherwise try to ignore the fact that they are actually breaking the rules themselves by chatting to each other when we are supposed to be listening to the teacher or getting on with our work'.

I won't endlessly go on with example after example, but you will get the gist of just why school rules can be an issue. I want to reiterate – these (real) examples may on the surface appear trivial, or petty. They are not. Causing confusion increases anxiety and risk to wellbeing, both in the short term and the long term, something to be avoided whenever possible.

Homework

It is not feasible to eradicate homework, much as I might like to. But it is possible to introduce some adjustments in relation to it. These include:

Ensure that homework is set with no ambiguity and appropriate guidance

Too many autistic pupils will react to homework in a way that puts them at a disadvantage that could be overcome with clarity of instruction. For example, guidance about how much writing would be appropriate is a simple method of ensuring that the individual doesn't either underestimate or overestimate how much he should be doing. Open-ended questions without limitations could prove problematic for an individual who could end up guessing as to what is expected of him. Having a level of clarity over what exactly is being asked for is also useful – ambiguous instructions are very unwelcome in the autism world, whereas any reduction in ambiguity would presumably benefit everyone.

Provide alternatives to doing homework at home

Sometimes it is simply impossible for parents to get their children to complete homework at home. For some, the association with school is too strong, and they are unable to consider doing school work in their safe environment. If you think that this isn't really much of a problem, think again. Too many autistic children associate school with being unsafe; if their only safe environment is at home, then it needs to remain that way. If having to complete homework at home means that the child then doesn't feel safe at home, it could be that they no longer have any safe space at all, which could be disastrous. All schools should ensure that there is time and space to complete work at school – before or after school, or during breaks.

Exams

I'm not a big fan of exams, and would go as far as to suggest that:

Whenever an examination is not required, it is replaced with a more suitable mode of knowledge transfer

I know – bit bold, isn't it? But I do wonder whether examinations in general really aren't particularly useful for anyone, let alone autistic pupils. There may be occasions in which an exam really is the only option in life (for example, a practical exam such as a driving test), but within education it becomes apparent that often the higher the educational 'standard', the less requirement there is for exams in the way that they are set at secondary school. For example, many degrees, post graduate degrees and doctorates won't include exams that are similar to those taken prior to going to university. If knowledge transfer can be completed by, for example, coursework in lieu of an exam, then perhaps that is a viable option during school as well as in higher education. If, however, in the interim we are looking for perhaps less dramatic adjustments (and let's face it, I don't think exams are going to be cancelled overnight), then we need to reflect on the following:

Language

In a similar vein as the musing above around homework, exams need to be written in a way that doesn't disadvantage an autistic pupil who may 'read' an exam question in the 'wrong' way due to its wording. This may not be the fault of the student – but it certainly disadvantages them unless there is flexibility in the marking of the question, which there often isn't. An adjustment might be:

All exam questions are reviewed by a panel of autistic adults to ensure that they are fit for purpose

When taken

There could be so much more flexibility in the educational system around when students in general can take their exams. Some schools are better than others at 'allowing' or encouraging students to take exams either earlier than is usual or later. I am a huge fan of reducing pressure on students and the massive emphasis that there is on chronological age and when exams are 'supposed' to take place. If we changed our cultural perspective on age and knowledge and it became more common for folk of all ages simply to take qualifications when they are ready rather than the more prescriptive ways that are generally expected, then it could suit a lot of people. Reducing the necessity of exams would also help in this process. Currently, all students sitting the same exam must do so at the same time to avoid any chances of questions being leaked. If exams were not the choice of knowledge transfer, then there would be a reduced necessity for students to be synchronized in their undertakings. Coursework is the obvious example, whereby students could complete coursework within set times and submit when they are ready.

Where taken

Some students find sitting exams in a large hall alongside lots of other students distracting to the point of disadvantage. There are some students who already have reasonable adjustments to provide alternatives, but there needs to be greater flexibility and more scope for autistic students who have very specific requirements at exam time. Having a scribe, additional time, alternative venues, typing rather than writing, are all examples of reasonable adjustments that could be considered.

Communication

Here are some suggestions for improving communication within a school setting.

Questions can be asked in a variety of different formats and at different times

Samantha absolutely loves her new school. She is an inquisitive girl who seeks answers to many things that she is learning about. But she is terrified of others looking at her whenever she asks a question in front of the class, to the point that it very rarely happens. Even when she does pluck up the courage to ask a question in front of the class, she is subsequently exhausted as it takes so much out of her. However, her new school provides different options to ask questions; for example, the teachers make it clear that as the teaching also appears in a live stream, students can use the message function to ask questions. Not only can they do that, but they can anonymize the question or even ask the teacher direct, which means that Samantha doesn't need to worry in the slightest about being the centre of attention.

Phil has excellent processing abilities – to the point that he often processes information well after the lesson has ended. This sounds oxymoronic. Allow me to explain. Phil not only has the ability to process the teacher's voice, but also processes all sorts of other sensory information that is going on around him – visual, olfactory, tactile, as well as auditory. As a result, even though he processes information at a faster rate than his peers, the sheer volume of what he processes means that he is often behind those who only process what they are hearing – specific to the teacher's voice. This puts Phil at a huge disadvantage as he only comes up with questions after the lesson has finished. However, being 'allowed' to contact his teacher to ask questions when they arise after he has had time to process information means that he is no longer at a disadvantage.

All teaching comes in different formats

Continuing on from Samantha's example above – all teaching is live streamed with a subtitle option, and recorded. For Angela, this is an absolute game changer. She is far better able to absorb information if she reads it rather than listens to it, so the subtitles mean that her learning ability is much more effective than it would otherwise be. Having the teaching recorded also means that she can watch over again when she feels the need to include pauses while she makes notes, as this really helps her to remember key points.

Headphones are a common feature in the classroom

Samantha and Angela's classmate, Agatha, also enjoys watching the teaching on the livestream. She chooses to have the subtitles off as she finds them a distraction – she finds lots of things distracting, in fact, so being allowed to wear headphones as she listens to the live stream provides her with an excellent way of drowning out extraneous noise and to focus just on the teacher's voice.

Focus equipment is not only allowed but encouraged

Some people used to call them fidget toys, which I find a bit patronizing. I really like the new term of focus equipment – and the fact that not only are they 'allowed' but they are encouraged! It's made a massive difference to my learning. Remember all that hype when hand spinner fidgets were banned from school because the consensus was that they would be distracting? Well, let me tell you, those and similar focus equipment do the opposite for me. They allow me to focus – the clue is in the name!

Classroom plan

Suggested adjustment:

Seating is allocated based on the needs of the student

It may seem like an innocuous thing, but the seating plan of a classroom could make all the difference to the student. The following are all aspects that might need to be taken into consideration:

- Whether the student is near someone else
- If they are in between others
- What the lighting looks like from their seat
- If they are near a window/door
- Are they at the front of the class or back
- How close they are to the nearest door.

Teaching and learning

Some of these, I accept, are less likely to be seen as reasonable – for example, the adjustments I suggested in the start of the chapter. They still have the potential to improve the educational experience for the autistic student, though, as well as reduce discrimination – and, after all, it's healthy to have a goal to work towards:

Certain subjects are taught with elements of autism-specificity as and when required

There are some subjects that require a far greater attention to autistic needs such as PSHE lessons, which would be better off being taught in alternative groups rather than whole classes. It is imperative that the right information around non-standard teaching is imparted in a manner most conducive to the learning style of autistic students. I did some research around offending behaviour, and so many of the case studies suggested that had appropriate learning taken place in school around things like what offending behaviour is, or what is meant by informed consent, then there would have been very different outcomes for the autistic adult. I will therefore add another adjustment:

As well as more standard sex and relationships education within PSHE lessons, additional information pertinent to autistic students is covered within appropriate groups

In order that teaching is productive, I believe that three components need to be fulfilled prior to engagement, and that all involved have similar levels of:

1 Communication style and ability
2 Motivation
3 Intellectual and cognitive abilities.

I genuinely think that there are some areas of information that are imperative to support autistic students (and others) as part of their journey into adulthood, and areas such as relationships and crime are so important that they warrant particular attention. Unless everyone in the group is 'on the same page' in aligning with the three points above, then it is likely that one or more in the group will miss out. This is why I feel that, in all likelihood, smaller groups compared to a traditional class size are required. Within the intense constraints of school life, this might not seem reasonable – unless one then considers the potential impact on the young person going into adulthood. Criminality (including offences relating to relationships) simply has to be covered in order to protect the autistic individual – either as a victim or as a perpetrator. While there are varying opinions on statistics, what is generally agreed is that an autistic person is far more likely to come into contact with the police; therefore, learning about why this might be and how to avoid it by reducing risk of being either a victim or perpetrator should absolutely be within the realms of reasonable.

Students have far greater say in which subjects they choose to study

Having as wide a ranging curriculum as possible, maybe even sharing courses between schools, to allow for greater flexibility with opt-in options as well as opt-out options to best suit the interests of students could increase educational opportunities all round.

Students can study subjects in blocks

As noted earlier, this may not strictly ever be seen as a reasonable adjustment, but it does seem to me to be something to aspire to. If a pupil has the sort of monotropic* brain that finds it difficult (or, indeed, impossible) to switch attention from one subject to another in a short timeframe, then expecting them to keep up with the myriad changes over a school day could be asking for the unattainable. If a student can happily focus on

---

*For more information on monotropism it is useful to start off with accessing https://monotropism.org/

one subject for long periods of time, however, then could it be considered reasonable to allow her to do just that? I love the idea of teaching even one subject at a time for however long it takes to succeed – and then moving on to the next.

There is an autodidactic offer for those who prefer it

Having the ability to learn autodidactically – solo learning – is not the sole domain of autistic students, nor is it the case that all autistic students are autodidactic learners. However, for those who are, there should be the option of choosing solo learning as a preferred learning opportunity in order that they have the best possible chance to succeed.

Lunchtimes and breaktimes

The clue is in the names – breaktimes are all about having a break and lunchtimes are a combination of having lunch and then a break. And yet for too many children, it is these interim times between lessons that can cause so much distress. Not having the downtime necessary to 'recover' from lessons only exacerbates non-regulation, so it is imperative that all students are well looked after during these periods of time and that they have the time and space to allow them to feel safe and enjoy some time to relax. Some suggestions include:

Breaktimes include alternative options for safe spaces

My last school was such a nightmare. Breaks were regulated to the point that it felt like being released from your cell to enter the 'yard' and all the stress that that entails. It was so regimented, so dictatorial, no choice. It really did feel like a 'release and return' process governed by the hideous bell sounding its knell at the start and end of the ordeal. And ordeal it was. Once out of the school building it was a real 'fend for oneself' kind of atmosphere with no escape. I used to go to bed dreading the next day and wake up in the morning with the same feeling. Ironically enough, I really like learning, and the lessons at school suited me just fine. But the bits in between – those memories will stay with me forever, much as I'd like to forget them.

My new school, on the other hand, is like living in absolute luxury. There are spaces within the school building, always with a watchful eye of a member of staff, with super clear rules about noise and conduct that are well adhered to. So, if I want to chill in the library in silence I can; if I want to have a quiet one-on-one game with my best friend, there is a classroom dedicated to that. Those with a disposition for the crowds can still go out, and they get whatever they get from that – while I enjoy some quiet time feeling safe in my own little sanctuary.

Lunch is offered in a variety of different spaces, including solitary spaces

I simply cannot abide eating in front of other people. I can't handle anyone looking at me when I'm eating; it causes too much anxiety, I feel like I can't swallow, and I end up choking. It literally means that I can't eat, so I go without. If only I was allowed to eat beyond prying eyes, that would make all the difference to me. They tell me 'no one is looking at you, don't worry, it's all fine' – which is clearly untrue and unfair and totally unempathic to me, which just makes me feel useless and worthless and stupid – and really, really hungry.

Eating with hands is a standard practice and food is offered in self-appointed receptacles

This school is quite simply awesome. I've never known anything like it. The laid-back approach to eating means that for the very first time in my life, I can eat at school without stress – which is phenomenal. It's just so unusual! They deliberately serve foods every day that are traditional dishes from around the world that are served without any cutlery because the traditional way of eating those dishes is with one's hands. This seems to have created an incredible culture, almost like 'anything goes', which then means that my preferences basically go unnoticed. We are not just allowed but encouraged to bring in our own plates, bowls and so on, if we feel more comfortable eating out of them – which is exactly what I do. So I get to bring my favourite bowl, my favourite spoon and still join in with what everyone else is eating, and I just don't stand out. Actually, it might surprise you just how many of the kids here also bring in their own stuff! I know someone else who has a real thing about food touching on a plate, and what she brings in is so cool. It's basically a platter with individual tapas-style clay pots that she can fill with whatever she wants to eat, without any risk of her dishes coming into contact with each other – it's not what I'd go for, but you can tell that she loves it.

Autistic eating requirements are taken just as seriously as other dietary ones

Schools take dietary requirements into account when it comes to health issues such as allergens. However, it is far less likely for a school to take autism-specific requirements into account – for example, the need for very soft food only or for food of a specific colour. My suggested adjustment is a genuine one. For children with potential reactions, it is clearly a health concern, which is why schools will adhere to the need for preparing individual plates for those who require it. But for the autistic child who *needs* certain requirements in order to be able to eat, then surely this is also a health concern that needs to be taken seriously. Not eating at all is, presumably, quite a major health concern for a young person. And not eating might place an individual at a substantial disadvantage.

Information systems (pupil passports and similar)

All autistic students have their key primary needs identified and highlighted to all teaching staff on a daily basis

This is based on the excellent doctoral thesis by Dr Julia Leatherland, who came up with the original concept of Facts About Me (FAMe™). The premise is that students have key needs identified that they want teachers to know about them, and then for those needs to be highlighted on the daily register. The joy of this system is that the needs are led by the students, and the register means that there is a very quick and easy reference point for staff to remind themselves what each individual student might need. So, for example, if a student finds it easy to concentrate while rolling a piece of putty in their fingers, then the teacher is alerted not to bring attention to this and to allow her to continue with that practice. What is essential as part of this process is that the person enabling the identification of needs has expertise in engaging with autistic students in the first instance, otherwise there is a risk that the system won't work.

5

Interventions

- All those involved with the child are cognizant at all times that the child is autistic
- Once one understands that the child is autistic, their autism is subsequently taken into account
- All nine questions on the ethics of intervention are considered prior to any intervention being agreed

'Autism interventions' – this always worries me, just in relation to the phrase itself. What exactly is being 'intervened' with? I absolutely understand the necessity of engaging with children to avoid harm, and to best increase chances of success for that child. However, I am not at all convinced, all of the time, that so-called interventions *do* have the best interests of the child in mind. There are any number of interventions that you can look up, and many profess to have positive outcomes. I'm not suggesting that any of these are good, bad or indifferent – what I do suggest is that a reasonable adjustment or, in this case, possibly reasonable considerations could make a huge difference on the outcomes for a child. The following nine questions form a framework that I have created that could easily be undertaken; the purpose of the framework is to generate thoughts around whether or not any particular intervention is suitable for the child.

Whenever engaging with a child, we are, in a sense, intervening. Even the act of deliberately *not* engaging with a child could be seen as a form of intervention. Any communication, interaction, engagement of any sort with a child could come under the umbrella of interventions – so where should we be drawing the line? Well, in an ideal world, we would be taking due consideration at all times around what might be best for the child, so maybe it's not a case of drawing any lines at all. One aspect that could be considered a reasonable adjustment, and one that I think is essential, is that:

All those involved with the child are cognizant at all times that the child is autistic

This might seem obvious, but you might be surprised just how often it is not taken into account. And my argument strongly suggests that not making this adjustment would potentially put the child at a substantial disadvantage, so really, I feel that it's a no-brainer. Being autistic means that you *do* need to engage in different ways at times – often, a lot of the time – if the child is not going to be put at a disadvantage. Being aware at a conscious level that the child is autistic therefore is a necessity to ensure that due consideration has taken place around the child's needs. Far too often, one might hear comments in relation to a child, for example at school, when the immediate and obvious (to the parent) response is 'well of course, but you've not taken their autism into account'. This can be not only distressing to parents and children alike, but it can also really increase the risk of harm to the child.

Parent: May I ask, again, why it is that you've asked me to be here today?

Teacher: Yes, of course. It's Isabelle, I'm afraid. She's insisted yet again on walking around the edge of the room on her way to her chair in the classroom, which takes her longer than if she went straight there and we think it annoys the other children.

Parent: I'm sorry – didn't I come into school last week to discuss this very thing?

Teacher: Yes, you did, indeed. Which is why we are even more concerned that it's still happening.

Parent: But as I explained last week, I won't tell her that she needs to go straight to her seat. As I explained to you, part of Isabelle being autistic is that her proprioception sensory needs are such that she has to run her hand along a wall in order to feel safe getting from A to B.

Teacher: Well, I don't know about all of that. None of the other children have a problem getting to their seat ...

Parent: No, I'm sure they don't. Are any of them autistic?

Teacher: Well, that's not relevant, we are talking about Isabelle here, and we must give her a consistent message ... so, are we agreed that we can *consistently* tell Isabelle that – just like all the other children – she needs to stop going the long way round to her seat?

Parent: I really don't think that she's going the long way around as such – as I've said, she *needs* to feel safe walking along the side of the wall. It's a bit like a blind person needing an uncluttered walkway to feel safe ...

Teacher: Yes, but Isabelle isn't blind, is she?!

Parent: Er, no – she's autistic, and as I said, she needs ...

Teacher: What she needs is to learn that she can't just do things her own way all the time ...

Ok – so this conversation could go on. Indeed, some of you reading may be wincing at how familiar it sounds. By the way, this is an example to make a point – I am fully aware that most teachers would never engage with a parent like that; unfortunately, the parental experience suggests that there are still some who do.

The point to be made from the above is the lack of conscious understanding from the teacher's perspective that Isabelle needs to have a different way of moving about as a direct result of being autistic. The teacher, even when prompted, is still refusing to accept that Isabelle's needs might differ and is trying to treat her in the same way as any other child in the class. This is such a common scenario, and one which absolutely must be addressed to ensure that the Isabelles of the world are afforded the same rights as anyone else to feel safe and secure. Is it reasonable that Isabelle gets to her seat in a way that makes her feel safe? Is it reasonable to expect the teacher to 'allow' her to do so? One would argue that the answer to both questions is a 'yes', and if the teacher was fully cognizant of Isabelle being autistic then they might have reacted differently. Or would they? An additional reasonable adjustment might then be:

Once one understands that the child is autistic, their autism is subsequently taken into account

This adjustment is an essential add-on to the previous one, otherwise there is a danger that an understanding that the child is autistic is not enough. The former adjustment is related to the knowing, the latter is related to the doing.

An overarching suggestion relating to the following nine questions:

All nine questions on the ethics of intervention are considered prior to any intervention being agreed

So, each of the following is a question that could be asked within a framework to identify the pros and cons of engaging with an autistic child, specific to what society tends to refer to as 'interventions'. Each question is posed as one that could (or should) be asked as a reasonable adjustment. In other words, I am arguing that asking the questions is a reasonable adjustment, and not asking them could lead to a substantial disadvantage. I have provided a brief rationale for each of the nine.

1 Is the intervention developed directly with the best interests of the autistic person at its core?
2 Does the intervention see the individual as an autistic person or someone who needs to be 'less autistic'?
3 What potential impact might the intervention have on the autistic individual?
4 What impact might the intervention have on those associated with autism (e.g. parents, carers, professionals)?
5 Is the main purpose of the intervention to directly or indirectly influence quality of life for the autistic person/population?
6 Does the intervention intend to establish new knowledge that can influence practice that will have a positive influence within the autism community?
7 How might the intervention enable practitioners to develop better practice?
8 How involved is the autistic individual in the aim/s of the intervention?
9 Does the intervention fulfil or acknowledge any criteria identified by the autistic person as needing change?

Is the intervention developed directly with the best interests of the autistic person at its core?

This sounds a little daft in a sense – but trust me, it's very real and very relevant. Far too many interventions do not take the best interests of the individual child into account. They either focus on the interests of others (for example, other family members) or they might suggest that the intervention 'worked' well for another child with the subsequent assumption that it will be equally effective, in the same way, for *your* child. Interventions *have* to take individual best interests into account at all times, otherwise there is a danger of the child being compromised and, therefore, disadvantaged.

Does the intervention see the individual as an autistic person or someone who needs to be 'less autistic'?

This is in line with narrative elsewhere about ableism and neuronormativity. Some organizations over the years have actually advertised their interventions as resulting in the child being 'less autistic' as an aim and a claim. Some of these assertions are misplaced, others are more sinister. An example of the former might be when an intervention claims to have led to a child going from being pre-verbal to verbal – alongside the claim that this, in and of itself, means that the child is less autistic. It doesn't mean that at all – the pre-verbal autistic child has simply transitioned into a verbal autistic child, simple as that. The more sinister side, of course, is when an intervention *seeks* to somehow make a child less autistic because their viewpoint is that being less autistic is a desirable state.

What potential impact might the intervention have on the autistic individual?

This is absolutely crucial to take into account and needs to be divided into three temporal zones: the immediate impact that the intervention may have on the child, the impact that the intervention might have over the course of the intervention, and the potential long-term impact. Here is an example based on a real-life scenario in which a primary school wanted to use a reward chart to try to get an autistic child to behave more in line with his PNT peers.

Tony was tasked with a number of goals – incidentally, none of which was designed for, nor agreed to, by Tony. The goals included not interrupting when the teacher was calling out names for registration; not moving in circle time while sat on the floor with the other children; and engaging in what the teacher called 'good listening', which entailed her reading from a book and checking to see whether the children were all paying attention (which she correlated with them looking at her while she read).

Tony's reality is that he found all of these things difficult – all for very good reason. He had learned, very specifically, to respond to the teachers when she read out the register. He had very distinctly and memorably heard her explicitly say: 'respond by saying "here" whenever I read out your names from the register'. Tony deduced – rightly so, in a sense – that he should respond with the required 'here' whenever any name was read out. After all, the teachers had asked for a response to your names (plural) not your individual name (singular). While in circle time, Tony has a distressing reaction to being touched by anyone, so is constantly trying to position himself in a manner that allows him to remain in circle time (as requested) but at the same time preserves his own safety by not having to touch another child. And being monotropic, Tony finds it very difficult to listen to words being spoken unless he is looking at something neutral and not distracting, such as a blank bit of carpet.

The response to Tony not behaving in a manner that was set out by the intervention meant that his own individual 'reward' chart – which was on display to everyone in that classroom – was actually more often than not in the negative. Tony's face was placed on the chart 'starting' in the middle, with down being negative behaviour (according to the intervention) and up being positive. The reward at the top of the chart, which was analysed on a day-to-day basis, was agreed with his parents: he would be allowed to choose a dessert after his evening meal.

The immediate impact on Tony was that he felt punished for simply being himself, and behaving in a manner that was natural and authentic. He responded as usual whenever anyone's name was read out in accordance with the teacher's original instructions, he kept himself safe in circle time, and he studiously paid attention to the teacher reading by staring at the floor.

The impact over the course of the intervention was that Tony not once got to choose a dessert at home after his evening meal.

The long-term impact of the intervention is that Tony grew to distrust school, withdraw from it, and refuse to speak to teachers, and faced numerous informal exclusions. He eventually ended up on the local authority register as a named 'school refuser'.

Who knows what the even longer-term implications might be?

This example might sound like exaggeration, but it's not. So many adults recount similar situations and just how traumatic they found them. This question suggested as a reasonable adjustment obviously takes some other questions into account – which is a demonstration as to why the questions need to be treated as a framework, not just as individual questions in their own right.

What impact might the intervention have on those associated with autism (e.g. parents, carers, professionals)?

This is a question to deliberately ensure that the impact on others aligns with the needs of the autistic child themselves. Sometimes, when going through the framework, it becomes apparent that the intended impact on others is, in fact, in direct contrast to what is best for the autistic child.

Is the main purpose of the intervention to directly or indirectly influence quality of life for the autistic person/population?

Surely it sounds reasonable to take autistic quality of life into account when engaging with the autistic person or the wider autistic population. It seems almost obscene to suggest anything else. And yet history shows categorically that this is not always the case. The fact that some interventions not only do not take autistic quality of life into account, but that they also proactively make the individual's quality of life considerably worse is both astonishing and distressing. Sometimes this might come from a position of faith – that the intervention does intend to improve quality of life. But there is misguided belief in changing behaviour to be in line with what the PNT perceive as behaviour that reflects quality of life; and that is where the problem lies. Taking the above example into account for the sake of simplicity. The teacher believes that a child's quality of life will improve if he listens to the teacher telling a story. The teacher also believes that the child demonstrates attention via his behaviour. And the teacher believes that the behaviour that denotes attention is where the child is looking. So, the consequences of this belief system is that the teacher tries to change the child's behaviour (looking at her when she is reading a story) with the faith that success in this area will lead to a reverse chain that benefits the child. In other words, that looking leads to attention, which leads to a happier child. However, when applied to Tony, the teacher's thinking is flawed – he is already enjoying listening to the story, and changing his behaviour to enforce looking would actually result in a decrease in his quality of life.

Does the intervention intend to establish new knowledge that can influence practice that will have a positive influence within the autism community?

This is somewhat a step removed from the impacts an intervention might have on the individual, but it is important nonetheless when it comes to the concept of reasonable adjustments. The argument is that unless knowledge can be developed, the autistic population will continue to be at risk of disadvantage. Therefore, any opportunity to increase real knowledge that influences the autistic and autism community for the better is an opportunity that should be taken.

How might the intervention enable practitioners to develop better practice?

Similar to the above, any intervention should have at least the potential to influence practice for the better – and by 'better', I mean better for the autistic child. It seems eminently reasonable to ensure that taking every possible step to improve practice is a key component of any autism intervention, seeing as it is ever so clear that current practice is a long way off from being effective across the autistic population.

How involved is the autistic individual in the aim(s) of the intervention?

It might be difficult to gain an accurate reflection of the 'autistic voice' – in other words what the child actually thinks and needs and wants. This doesn't suggest that we don't make every effort available to do exactly that. It is astonishing – not in a good way – just how many times interventions are applied to or forced on an individual without anyone actually doing what they can to involve the individual in the process itself.

Does the intervention fulfil or acknowledge any criteria identified by the autistic person as needing change?

Perhaps this should have been the first question to pose within the framework, as it is pertinent to take into account before progressing at all! In a similar vein to the previous question, there has to be an effort to find out whether the autistic child himself actually feels that he wants to change anything in his life and, if so, why. Equally as valid is if the child *doesn't* want anything to change; is there an authentic reason for this justification to be upheld? So, a very simple example again taken from the above, might be that Tony really wants to listen to his teacher reading a story and, therefore, doesn't want anyone to try to force him to look at her while she is reading. In this instance, it is obvious that Tony makes a remarkably good point, and that the intervention of the reward chart should not expect him to change that facet of his behaviour. Similarly, Tony has the right to not feel in physical distress – so not only should he be 'allowed' to wriggle about to ensure that he is not touching another child, there should be proactive, preventative measure put in place on his behalf to stop it happening in the first instance. Finally, the wording of when a child responds to names being called out at register time needs adapting to avoid any linguistic ambiguity.

6

The autistic profile

- That society understands the different types of energy and that they all have their own significance relating to an individual being able to engage
- The 3 'R's of recognition, regulation and resilience in relation to autistic energy are taken into account at all times
- Understand that autistic masking may differ from the PNT masking behaviour
- Understand the links between autistic masking and trauma
- Always reflect on whether it is wise to encourage masking – who is it for?
- Never insist on masking when it is not needed
- Autism is understood within the model of a constellation, taking time and environment into account

Reasonable adjustment suggestion:

That society understands the different types of energy and that they all have their own significance relating to an individual being able to engage

Energies

Most people have a good understanding of energy as a concept, and almost everyone will have a good understanding when you say that you're tired and you want to go to bed.

Equally, people will appreciate it when, while out for a walk, you say that you're feeling tired so you would like to complete the walk and go and rest. Why is it, then, that being tired in relation to physical energy is so easily taken into account, but it is so very much harder for autistic children to be given any freedom whatsoever in recovering when their energy levels are so low? In my book *What Works for Autistic Adults*, I developed a list of nine different types of energy, which are:

1 Social
2 Communication
3 Physical
4 Mental
5 Sensory
6 Processing
7 Emotional
8 Situational
9 How energy links together.

My point is that if your child went to school and there was a PE lesson that involved a cross-country run, and she came with a note and photo saying, 'Please excuse Charlotte as she completed the London Marathon yesterday; here is her finisher photo with her wearing her medal', I don't suppose that for one moment the school would not comply with your request. And yet are any of the other, equally as valid, types of energy taken into account along with the various expectations of your child?

I will briefly go through the above types of energy with an example of each one in relation to reasonable adjustments.

Social

Richard is his own unique sociality as an autistic child in that he is deeply interested in the right people. On a daily basis, he can quite easily engage with life so long as the social side of things doesn't get out of hand. What leads to it getting out of hand, however, is exposure to other children who fall outside of his comfort zone. Richard finds social rules, which after all remain 'unwritten', a complete mystery – so having to engage with PNT children with their own set of rules leads to social exhaustion almost every day. School becomes so problematic that Richard spends all of his 'spare' time – evenings and weekends – socially exhausted, which means he has no energy to do anything else. Seeing as Richard also likes to be on the move, not being able to expend physical energy leads to his being far too awake at night to sleep properly, which has the obvious knock-on effect of being exhausted the next day. Being exhausted the next day means that he starts the morning with a much-depleted energy store ... and the cycle starts all over again.

If those around him recognized that Richard is *not* unsociable – which is the label that he has been branded with – but realized that his sociability included just a select number of individuals, and they not only allowed but encouraged Richard to engage with those children during breaktime at school, then his social energy would actually increase. Richard *gains* energy from these like-minded individuals. All of a sudden, Richard would no longer be exhausted at the end of the school day, and his life would turn around immediately for the better.

Communication

Gemma has an excellent linguistic ability and a fast-moving brain. She is forever evolving her ideas around topics that interest her and eagerly engages with others to let them know what her thoughts are. However, others with whom Gemma communicates often criticize her. They tell her that she is a 'know-it-all' who thinks she's right 'all of the time'. The result of this is that, over time, she becomes more and more reluctant to share her thoughts, and eventually trains herself to stop conversing about what is important to her, concentrating only on what other people think is important. This is devastating to Gemma, as it shuts off a whole range of communications that resonate with her and give her a reason to live.

The reality is that Gemma is neither a 'know-it-all', nor does she claim that she is right 'all of the time'. However, she **does** know her topics in a vastly superior way to her peers and is far more advanced in her thinking and reasoning. As a result of the latter, she feels a deep sense of distress that she is being belittled and accused for thinking she is right all of the time; her reality is that she absolutely recognizes her own fallibility and is always keen to be demonstrated incorrect – it is her way of learning. Equally, however, Gemma is such a deep thinker that she would rarely, if ever, say anything that she had not put a great deal of thought into, so she won't say anything that she isn't at least reasonably confident will be correct. It troubles her that this is even raised as an issue, as she had always assumed that **everyone** puts the same degree of thought into their communications and finds it difficult to understand why anyone wouldn't. Gemma finds the criticisms against her hurtful and damaging, to the point at times of feeling soul-destroyed that people around her dismisses her voice so apparently and easily.

If Gemma was understood through her own authentic lens (and was allowed to develop her own authenticity in a safe environment), then the story may be very different, with potentially massively opposite outcomes. If Gemma grew up knowing that she communicated differently – no, scrap that; if Gemma grew up knowing that *others* communicated differently to her (a subtle, perhaps, but important distinction), and what those differences might be, she may grow up confident, willing (and able) to continue her inquisitive journey of discovery long into the future. Simply, a different understanding and different reactions to Gemma could mean the difference between squashing a child's curious nature and allowing a child to evolve into a Nobel prize winner.

Physical

I don't think that physical energy should be mentioned in this context without making mention also of fatigue. I will be writing about burnout later but for the moment I will focus on fatigue.

Erica's parents simply didn't understand just what a close relationship there was between anxiety and fatigue and, subsequently, Erica being so tired all the time. They kept on with the suggestions that they had been given by the healthcare professionals, to no avail. In reality, it is hardly surprising as they originally 'only' asked for information about how to encourage a child to get a good night's sleep. The problem for Erica, though, wasn't so much that she was not getting enough sleep – it was the fact that her levels of anxiety were so consistently high that she felt fatigued all the time, which led to brain fog, incoordination and a pervasive sense of being inferior to her peers. Left unchecked this could have had dire consequences for Erica in the long term.

On discovering that Erica was autistic, Erica's parents began to work out what the real problem was. Working backwards, with some help from their local autistic adult forum – who were only too happy to relate Erica's experiences to their own as children – Erica's parents realized that without any way to regulate her anxiety (or even recognize it in the first instance), Erica's anxiety culminated in ongoing fatigue that no amount of sleep would combat. Her parents realized that, in the short term, identifying key areas of anxiety (for her it was PE lessons at school, along with transport to and from school, that really caused her acute anxiety) and removing those (being excused from PE, and parents taking her instead of using the school bus) immediately had an impact on her anxiety. This didn't lift the fatigue straight away, but it did reduce it to a level by which Erica was much better able to think through her own state of being and be far more cognizant of what caused her anxiety – which in turn allowed her to identify additional things in her life that required change.

Mental

Luca's cognitive processing can vary hugely depending on the way in which information is delivered to his brain. For example, if presented with a book, he processes pages of text very slowly as he gets easily distracted by the book itself; by the fact that there are two pages open at any given time; that he has no control over the size of font of the text; while the feel of the book also invades his cognitive space. Luckily, his teaching assistant has a great deal of empathy and is more than willing to let Luca borrow his iPad, which has an app on it that can download books for the user to read. The app allows the reader to have control over all sorts of functions, including the size, colour and font of the text. The fact that Luca can adjust the text to a way that suits his cognitive style means that he reads twice as fast and retains twice as much information compared to when he is reading a physical book.

Sensory

Sensory hell: being dragged around the supermarket. It's autism hour – so supposedly a time that suits me – but it's not enough for me. The lights are still too bright; autism hour doesn't mean that I don't suffer from the noise of the freezers, the absolute onslaught of visuals down each aisle makes my head spin, there are fluctuations in the temperature, the trolley has a wobbly wheel that keeps squeaking, the fish counter that Mum avoids because she knows how much it distresses me still distresses me from 20 feet away, I end up unable to speak and can only vote with my feet. I run. Escape. Another disaster, no shopping done; I'm a wreck, and Mum is quietly angry all the way home.

Sensory heaven: I sit, with Mum, and we take it in turns to click on the button to choose what to buy on the shopping app. Click, click, click. I'm in my onesie, the lights are dimmed, and we are snuggled up underneath the blanket. We have all the time in the world, no pressure, just the joy of being together and getting the job done. Quicker than a car trip out, for sure. No distress, no need for recovery time, just fun, fun, fun. Whoever invented online shopping – thank you.

Processing

Carl really struggles with rumination as a result of being overwhelmed with so much input during the school day; the problem with this is that he is frequently absolutely mentally buzzing when he goes to bed as he needs to process much of that input to make sense of it before he has to head back into the school the next day. By the time he has gone through what he needs to process, he has lost the opportunity to have a good night's sleep, so is very tired the next day when he has to repeat the cycle.

Carl is lucky in that he has a teacher who recognizes Carl's overwhelm and suggests some strategies to help alleviate what he has to process. He finds visual processing far easier than auditory processes, so the teacher makes sure that she always 'allows' him to watch his software that picks up her voice and provides instant subtitles. This not only allows Carl to process her voice easily, it also means that he is so focused on reading the subtitles that he is far less distracted by other stimuli, again reducing the need for him to get overwhelmed with processing information. He is able to get a good night's sleep from then on.

Emotional

It's good to have empathy.
I get that, I do.
Everyone says it, so
it must be true.
They tell me I lack empathy
– if only they knew.
I'm a hyper-empath,
I'm one of the few.
The problem is overwhelm,
Believe me, it's true.
I feel everything,
I feel all of you.
So I close down
That's what I do.
It's a necessity,
To get me through.
And you call me cold,
That is your view.
You are so, so wrong.
If only you knew.

Surely we know by now that rather than lacking in empathy, so many autistic individuals are incredibly emotionally empathic to the point of overwhelm. Emotions, and emotional overload, are a reality for many autistic people, and children in particular may find it hugely difficult to cope with processing all of their – and others' – emotions. Emotional energy can be incredibly giving at times – but it can also be incredibly draining.

Understanding that the child is a hyper-empath and no longer suggesting that she lacks in empathy can make the most extraordinary difference in the child's life. The new lens through which one understands the hyper-empathic child can be truly illuminating, and can provide a picture diametrically opposed to how she was previously viewed. The subsequent positive implications of this change in perspective are immense.

Situational

> *They just don't seem to get me. What's so difficult to understand? Just because I don't speak shouldn't mean that I don't have a voice. I've certainly got my opinions, if only they could stop misinterpreting them! They are always trying to figure out what the factors are that make a difference to me, why sometimes I am so overwhelmed that I can't cope, and at other times I'm in my element. What they don't seem to realize is that it is the specific situation that I am in that is the biggest influence of them all. The problem is that they seem to think that one shop is the same as another, that one doctor's setting is the same as the next one, that just because I love the hustle and bustle of a street market then I should also be able to enjoy the hustle and bustle of school assembly. I know – it's crazy when you think about it, but still, they just don't get it!*

How energy links together

Eve has a clear pattern of energy that she and her parents have figured out beautifully. Her energy relationships are charted and analysed so that each day there is a perfect blend of energies that means she is always fresh, always capable and always ready for bed. Between them, they have figured out that emotional energy is what takes much away from Eve, so her exposure to emotional situations is kept to a minimum. If she knows that she will be exposed to a situation in which it is likely that emotions will run high, then she allocates several days before and after to prepare and recover. She needs to expend a certain amount of physical energy, and they discovered that specific types of exercise have a huge positive impact on her cognitive processing and problem solving. A simple example being that monotonous exercise that doesn't take up much brain space massively increases her ability to problem solve at the same time. She has an up-to-date sensory profile that allows her and her parents to be measured when it comes to sensory exposure, and she tends to communicate online rather than in person when the situation allows. Overall, the three of them are hyper-aware of the blend of energies that are good for Eve; the impact that this has had on her life is an absolute game changer.

Recognition, regulation, resilience

This adjustment is all about society allowing for the first and second of the three (or, even better, determining how to *encourage* them) followed by a questioning of the necessity of the third. So, the adjustment being:

The 3 'R's of recognition, regulation and resilience in relation to autistic energy are taken into account at all times

In the first instance, recognition refers to recognizing what energies are at play in any given situation. Regulation – much like in the example provided by Eve above – is all about how to create a blend of energy that suits the child. And resilience is to be avoided at all costs. In other words, *having* to be resilient means that we are getting it wrong! The idea of 'building up resilience' is one that should be avoided.

> *Zoe has long since been exhausted by early afternoon at school. She finds that being exhausted massively limits her ability to think straight, which then impacts on her ability to work out what she needs to do to look after herself. This then compounds the issue as she often finds herself in situations that continue to deplete her energy levels so that by the time she gets home, she is in such a state of inertia that it is impossible for her to engage in any kind of activity that relaxes her. This happens every day, and the weekends are literally recovery time before facing the next week at school.*
>
> *On discovering the concept of the 3 'R's, she begins, with support from her parents and her teachers at school, to break down the day into sections. These are not always time-orientated; they are usually event-orientated. For example, one event is her transport to school, another is her first lesson and so on. For each one she keeps a simple scale that is specific to her on which she notes how many spoons she feels she has either gained or lost. She does this for a few days, and then shares her chart with her parents, who then discuss with her what she feels is specific within each event that leads to spoon movement. While it's not a 'science' with infallible results, this does start to allow Zoe and her teachers and family to begin to understand where the 'pinch points' are for her energy drain, and therefore gives her the opportunity to decrease*

some activities. This is the beginning of her regulation phase, and has the knock-on effect of Zoe subsequently being a lot brighter throughout the day and into the evening – which, ironically enough, actually gives her the chance to relax in the evening at home, which allows her to regulate even further. Even in a short space of time, the exercise allows Zoe and those around her to work out where she has been expected – unfairly (impossibly) – to be resilient, and to eliminate those activities until such a time that she is ready.

The above example is a fictitious one, as it happens – but is based on a number of individuals going through similar scenarios but merged together to make the point. I maintain that adopting the principle of the 3 'R's could be an effective adjustment that has a significant impact – in other words, reduces the chance of students who suffer from depleted energies to no longer be at a disadvantage.

Masking

Autistic masking is becoming more and more understood, but there is still a way to go. The following are suggestions in relation to masking (you can read extensively about autistic masking elsewhere):

Understand that autistic masking may differ from the PNT masking behaviour

I find it so frustrating when I try to explain my masking and what it means to me. Far too often, the response that I get is 'oh yes, masking. Well, we all do that, don't we? I mask loads – I'm forever putting on a front. I think it's just normal, to be honest.' This is, much of the time, gaslighting. I'm not saying that it always is, but whenever I've questioned people it turns out that what they mean by masking isn't anything to do with the experience that I have of masking. I think it ought to be renamed to avoid confusion. I think what most people think is masking – or, at least, is what they assume I mean when I talk about it – is them slightly altering their persona to meet the needs of any particular situation in which they find themselves. So far as I can tell, this bears very little resemblance to what I experience when I'm masking. I used to ask people, 'when you "mask", do you know you're doing it all the time? Does it take a real conscious effort, and do you need to recover afterwards?' The answers were almost always either 'no, no and no', or they would look at me uncomprehendingly, which tells its own story. My point is, when I mask – and I feel that I need to, a lot – I have to concentrate so hard to do so, my mind has to work overtime to do it, and I am absolutely mentally exhausted as a result. It's not at all uncommon for me to have to lie down – literally in a darkened room – if I've spent too much time in a situation in which I need to mask. I just wish everyone would stop pretending that everyone is like this – they are not. All it does is to belittle my experiences and make me feel even worse.

Understand the links between autistic masking and trauma

Years of masking have made it very difficult to engage in the so-called real world. Day after day, week after week, month after month, and – you guessed it – year after year of forcing myself to be someone else has left me bereft. Bereft of my authenticity, bereft of my lost childhood, bereft of my very soul. I can't go out without masking; it's so ingrained in me, and every time I mask it brings back all those years of torment, as if I am reliving them all over again. The stress, the shame of being not good enough, the utter belief that 'their' way of doing it was the only right way – so me, being me, meant being constantly in the wrong. Life is either a lonely, sad and broken existence behind my wall of despair, or a venturing out, triggering trauma each time I try, once again, to fit in. I see the younger ones on social media, 'proudly autistic', stim dancing and talking openly about their experiences and I am so happy for them. I can see a shadow of me in them, but also see what could have been. It could have been me, if only I had lived a different life, if only I had not been forced to mask, if only I had been allowed to be me.

Always reflect on whether it is wise to encourage masking – who is it for?

'I really think it would be better if you just conformed.' 'I honestly don't know why you have to always do it differently.' 'You do know how irritating it is when you say that?' All pretty obvious examples in my life which have, however well-meaning, led to me feeling that I need to do things in a different way. Different to my own, authentic, natural way of being. And why was I made to feel like that?

'I really think it would be better if you just conformed.' This – despite all the endless reports explaining that I was autistic, that the anxiety it caused me to break out of my way of doing things just to fit in with everyone else – had led to several breakdowns. Despite the fact that I was, at the tender age of 13, already well into my mental health pathway and on to my third therapist. And it was the therapist who actually said it to me: 'I honestly don't know why you have to always do it differently'.

*'Er – because I **am** different? It's the equivalent of asking the short person why they always have to jump a bit higher in order to reach the top shelf, or asking the left-handed person why they wrote in a different way,*

or asking the blind person why they insisted on using an audio book. Difference is ok – so why make me feel so awful for being different?'

You do know how irritating it is when you say that?' Irritating to whom, may I ask? And why is it so irritating to you, simply asking for clarification over an instruction that doesn't really mean very much to me? Is it irritating because I've pointed out that the instruction was ambiguous? Was it irritating because I've noted that my way of wording it would have been more effective and meaningful? If you're irritated because your wording wasn't very good, perhaps you should be irritated at yourself and do something about it, rather than be irritated with me.

Never insist on masking when it is not needed

'It's ok to be different. In fact, here we encourage it.' Those words, uttered to me after I had 'failed' in a couple of primary schools, changed my life forever. For the first time ever, I felt that I was being heard (in the right way), being seen (in the right way) and being allowed, encouraged to be me. I used to wish that I was invisible, that I never had to speak, that I could go under every radar that ever existed just to avoid the crushing comments about the way I spoke, the way I behaved, the fact that I was 'different'. I used to assume that being told that I was 'different' really meant that I was 'broken' or 'wrong'. Being accepted in this new school exactly for who I was put paid to all of that. It was, literally, a life-changing moment and, from that day on, I learned that it was ok to be me, and I should be proud to be different.

The autistic constellation

While the common term seems to be 'spectrum' when it comes to referring to autism, as noted, I am less than keen. More and more, people are starting to refer to the concept of the 'spiky profile', which is far better and more accurate. Taking it one step even further (and I claim no credibility for this – I believe that it was Caroline Hurst who first wrote about it and that others were talking about it at the time too), I feel that the following should be adopted:

Autism is understood within the model of a constellation, taking time and environment into account

The idea of a constellation is a brilliant one, as it is infinite in its application while at the same time applicable to any one given individual at any one time. One can choose which components one believes to be beneficial to understand circumstances that are unique to an autistic person, at any given specific time point. Using the model of energy above, combining it with other environmental facts and adding time into the equation, we can produce a model that can be extremely illuminating when understanding individual circumstances. We can produce a concept that is multi-dimensional – and rightly so. Autism does not exist in a vacuum, autism is not one-dimensional, and the impact of autism + environment will differ, depending on all the plethora of variables – and may also change over the passing of time.

It was once the case – and I'm speaking from experience of working in residential services here – that assessments of 'a person's autism' were based on the outdated model of autism, which dictated that autism was an issue around communication, social interaction and imagination. This did evolve to eventually include sensory issues. But this is all too simplistic when trying to understand the autistic experience in a meaningful way.

One of the reasons why I have such a preference for autism + environment = outcome is that it takes the onus away from addressing the 'autism only' component of what might impact a person. For far too long, any given individual has only been seen within the autism context – and, in a way, only if they were lucky to be identified in the first place. Autism is an essential component of the equation – but autism itself will be unique to the individual, and needs to be understood through that individual's unique lens. Then we have the environment, which can also be broken down into several sub-components. And then we have other aspects, such as the passing of time.

As an example of the complexities of the constellation model – which is also an indication of why it is such a useful one:

Autism needs to be part of the constellation – but can be broken down into dozens of different aspects, each of which will differ from one person to the next, for example processing different types of communication.

Environment needs to be part of the constellation – and I've broken down the environment into components, thus:

- Self
- Others
- Sensory
- Society – further broken down to:
  - values
  - attitudes
  - knowledge
- Policies/procedures
- Law/criminal justice system.

And, of course, each of the above can be broken down even further – for example, self can be broken down into any number of aspects, not least energies – of which I've identified nine ...

And so on, and on. The point is that this is why the idea of a constellation is both incredibly complex but also incredibly useful. After all, people *are* complex, and if we genuinely want to best understand a person, then buying into those complexities can only be a good thing.

> *All my life, all I've wanted is to be understood. All my life.
> I've been told 'it's something to do with communication'
> (from the speech and language therapist), 'it's your
> developmental delays' (child psychologist), dietary misuse
> (nutritionist), abnormalities in learning (education) ... I
> can't be bothered to list all the different professions who
> tried to dissect me and point out all the things that could
> be blamed for me being me. My gorgeous, understanding,
> accepting, empathic partner doesn't dissect me. They
> accept me for who I am, and embrace my personality and
> me, just for being me. It's all I ever wanted.*

7

Eating and drinking out

I've written this chapter in a slightly different way compared to the others, partly because I wanted to shoehorn my concept of Autopia (Autistic Utopia) into print. You could read it as a playful chapter, or – if you are serious about inclusion – you could read it as a possible guide to changes that could be made within the industry to genuinely effect change to better include autistic people.

Activities such as eating or drinking out (or both) can be fraught. Having to put up with systems that are simply meant to cater either for the majority of the customers or for the ease of use of the staff might mean that they are inappropriate for your and/or your child's needs. Added to that could be the issues of having to involve actual other people with the myriad stressors that that brings, and for some of you, it's simpler just not to go out. And yet you shouldn't be at a disadvantage in this area of life. Autopia suggests that there are some things that could change to make eating and drinking out more accommodating for you.

Website for an Autopian restaurant

About us

We know that many autistic families – families in which one or more of you are autistic – may, for many different and individual reasons, find it difficult to access the eating-out experience. Here, we feel that it is your basic human right to enjoy a meal out as an individual, a couple or a family, and we have done our best to accommodate you to facilitate that happening. Here are some of the things we can offer, based on our ongoing feedback from autistic families:

Having the place to yourself

We are aware that for some of you, there is no issue with eating out – so long as others are not around! To this end, we set aside days and nights during which we can allocate eating rooms entirely devoid of others – you will have the place to yourself. This includes your own entrance area so you should be able to relax with the full knowledge that you don't need to have to concern yourself about potential clashes with other diners.

Choosing your time of day/night to eat

We run 24-hour dining times to suit the more nocturnally orientated among you. Once you've chosen what time you would like to access our restaurant, we will guarantee that the table you have chosen is ready at exactly the time you have requested it.

Pre-ordering your food

We like to provide as much choice as possible, in order to cater for as many of our customers as we can. However, one downside to this is the fact that an extensive menu can be somewhat overwhelming at times. Our full menu is available to peruse at your own leisure, and we are happy for you to pre-order at a time that suits you. Just send your order in and there will no longer be any need to give your order in person on the day. We also provide miniature versions of all meals, so if you like an array of different tapas-style meals, then that option is open to you. Our size options are as follows:

- Bite size – as you might expect, this is a genuine single bite for taste purposes only.
- Miniature – think about the size of plate that an average cat might enjoy, about a sixth of the average-sized meal.
- Modicum – a good option for a child portion, but could easily be a side dish or part of a main meal – about a third of a portion.
- Medium – this is the largest of our small options, and comes in at roughly half a portion.

Plates, cutlery, glasses and other practical considerations
You may well have a preference, and there are links below to view all the ranges that are available. Simply click on the ones that best suit your needs and we will provide those. Feel free to mix and match if your family members like to utilize different plates! We are also aware that for some of you, nothing tastes quite right unless it is served within your own receptacle – in which case, feel free to bring yours along, and choose the 'serving dish only' option from the drop-down menu.

Choose your silence or sound
Sound is so important when eating – some of our diners love a bit of sound, others prefer as quiet an experience as possible. We have a range of options of music and different sounds, plus we have a series of Bluetooth speakers set around the dining area for you to link with if you wanted to bring your own sounds. We can also provide headsets if you are the kind of family who enjoy different, individual sound options while you are eating.

Self-service options
We love engaging with our autistic families but appreciate that sometimes it is our staff who can cause some

level of stress. If you have eaten with us before and enjoyed being served by a specific person then do let us know and we will do what we can to ensure that he/she/they will be available (we will let you know well in advance if this is not possible). However, we also have a self-serve option; as soon as you are ready for the next course to be prepared and delivered just press the buzzer and when your food is ready, the sliding hatch will open and you can help yourself to that course – you can eat out without having to speak to anyone but yourselves!

Bring your own food
While we pride ourselves on our food, we do realize that many of you might have a family member for whom nothing else but their own food, prepared in a unique way, will really do when it comes to mealtimes. If you are one of those families, no problem – you are welcome at our eatery, and you can either drop off the meal beforehand (with clear instructions as to how to prepare and serve it) or simply bring it with you on the day.

Pre/post payments
We offer a range of ways to pay for your experience, including options that avoid contact with staff in case that is something that is important to you – after all, who wants to have their meal spoiled at the end when you have to sort out calling for and paying the bill? If you have pre-ordered you can always pay before you even dine with us; alternatively, there are options to pay within 48 hours after you have dined with us. Let us know how you would like to be contacted (e.g. email or phone) with the final bill, then leave the rest to us.

Bring your own animal(s)

Finally, we have rooms available in which it may be possible for you to bring extended family members in the form of pets. Please check with us first! If your pets have specific needs, please do also chat to us about how we might best accommodate them.

Happy dining!

Can pubs do better?

After the recent Covid pandemic changed practice so dramatically, there are some aspects of said change that are exquisitely autism-friendly. The fact that many pubs now have an app whereby one can sit and order and pay for drinks without having to fight for one's right to be served at a bar is an excellent idea – and one which would be even better if it was a requirement rather than simply an option! Bring on pubs that welcome neurodivergent adults with a level of understanding, such as:

Paying
Use the app to order and pay.

I am amazed. For the first time – ever – I have been able to take the family out to a pub. My kids are fine when it comes to people around them, just not ok with having to watch their dad disappear into a group of people without any knowledge as to when I will return. We tried getting them to come with me but the stress of being told 'you're not allowed to have young children at the bar' was just too much. Now, however, we have an app that means we can order what we want from the comfort of our own table. This has the added bargain of the kids being able to see what is available for them to choose from. If you've got kids like mine, you'll know what I mean! Asking the open-ended question 'what would you like to drink' is a sure-fire way of quick-starting panic mode from which there is no return. And it's just not possible to guess what a pub might or might not have, and thinking they have something and then not being able to get it at the bar is also a swift departure to disaster land. I've never realized just how in love one person can be with a pub app – but I am that person, and I do love it.

Your drinks

Feel free to bring your own receptacle for drinking out of.

My child could be called fussy. In fact, others often do refer to her in this way. I resent this. I resent the fact that they judge her through their own, poor standards. I resent the fact that they don't understand just how important cleanliness is to her, and how important being able to drink out of her very own canteen isn't really a preference, it's a necessity. The comfort of it, the feel of it, the smell of it. Fluids are not the same out of anything else, so she won't drink them. Why can't they realize that it's more important for my beautiful daughter to drink than it is to try to force her to use a different receptacle? Don't they realize just how important drinking is to human welfare? Why do they seem to think that it's such a big deal that my daughter has discovered her perfect drinking experience and, quite understandably, wants to keep it?

Seating requirements

If you have any requirements about seating, please let us know and we can reserve your choice at the times you request.

Such a game changer. I remember those times when they didn't know that I was autistic, and I used to 'abscond' all the time. Well, that's the label the psychologist always used to give me in those endless sessions when my parents tried to find out what was 'wrong' with me. The psychologist – seemingly either unaware that I was in the room, or perhaps he just didn't think I was listening or couldn't understand, or just maybe, he didn't really care – used to tell my parents that I had 'absconding behaviour borne out of a wilful desire to grab attention' and that 'active ignoring' was the answer. The result being that I would enter an environment and be forced to sit at a table that I couldn't tolerate, however much I tried, until such a point when I knew that I would either have to leave – or have a meltdown there and then in the pub. Past experiences told me that the latter was too traumatic to ever repeat, so I would always have to escape. I would try to get my parents' attention by pulling their arms, or sliding my chair away, but their 'active ignoring' meant that they took no notice. Nowadays, of course, they know far better. After that last time when they decided that the dangers of me wandering around on my own outside the pub, looking in through the windows in the hope someone would rescue me, outweighed any kind of alternative plan, they knocked active ignoring on the head. From then on, they had the bright idea of 'letting' me choose the table. Which meant that I could always choose one right against a wall and as close as possible to the exit, so I always had the comfort of an escape route if I needed it. All this was a luxury – and now, the fact that we can book in advance means that we don't even have to face the disappointments of getting somewhere to find that the best table has already been taken. When I found my voice, I told my folks all about why I used to run, and they were absolutely mortified at how they had 'handled' me. I told them it wasn't their fault, but they still felt bad. I always reassure them these days that I love going out with them – just book that table first!

Noise

We understand that noise may be an issue – we very much welcome folk who opt for ear defenders, and we have an outdoor area in which we ask folk to be as quiet as possible, and there is a covered and heated area within that space too.

I play 'spot the ear defenders' whenever I go out. Not literally only ear defenders, anything that I think might indicate that someone else has a sensory need that I recognize. You'd be surprised at what you see these days, and it's always an absolute joy to know that I'm not alone. Of course, in this day and age where huge earphones are a basic prerequisite for cool teens, it's even better. Standing out wearing ear defenders in public used to completely stress me out. Now, with autism-friendly pubs where such things are an expected norm, I can go out without any fear whatsoever of feeling like I'm in the spotlight.

Toilets

There are outdoor toilets that are available to access via all doors, so there is no need to have to navigate the throngs.

It's a weird one, but I swear loads of people aren't bothered about going to the toilet. By which I mean they don't stress about it. I know – really strange! And yet for me and my mates, it's a constant source of chatter. Why we hate going to the toilet in public, the incredible things we've done (or, even, still do) to avoid going to the toilet, why no one else seems bothered – it's of great comfort to me to know that others get just as stressed as I do. One of the things we all agree on – and this is something that we've noticed that none of the professionals who talk about 'toileting' ever mentions – is the stress and strain of actually getting to the loo and back again in the first place. Plenty of us are so wrapped up in the complexities of having to navigate busy spaces, spaces fraught with danger, filled with people, plates, glasses and constant movement, that we do whatever we can to avoid needing the toilet. Some of us just sit miserably, refusing to have a drink to make sure we don't have to do anything with a full bladder. But this pub that I've found, purely by coincidence, has an outdoor toilet. Plus it has loads of exits from the main pub so you can get up, make your way easily to a door, and then it's pure open space to enjoy between you and the loo. It's absolute lavatorial heaven.

8

Language (again), health and social care, and sensory profiles

- Professionals should be led by the autistic community around terms relating to autism
- Communication options are a right
- Autism understanding needs to reflect autistic children's needs
- Professionals understand that autism is not a mental health condition
- Mental health conditions should be considered as potentially environmental and, therefore, could be alleviated outside of medication
- Therapy is adapted to meet autistic need
- Being autistic should not preclude support in any other area
- Behaviour needs to be understood within an autism context
- Sensory profiles and audits must be ongoing and up to date
- A & E settings are usually autism-unfriendly; provide alternatives where possible
- Research on Fabricated or Induced Illness (FII) is imperative

I've written elsewhere about the reduction of anxiety within health settings, and I don't want to simply repeat myself. Amalgamating professionals together, though, some of the adjustments are as pertinent to one profession as they are to any other. I am very aware that the supreme Dr Mary Doherty is leading the way in relation to what needs to change within health settings, and I would encourage anyone interested in inclusive autism practice to look up her work. I have chosen just some examples of potential adjustments for the rest of the chapter with adjoining narratives as explanations. As noted, please do also take a read of how to reduce anxiety in, for example, Avoiding Anxiety in Autistic Adults.

Professionals should be led by the autistic community around terms relating to autism

Language

I've already written about how important language is, and I won't rehash those ideas. Here are some more examples, though, of why language matters so much, and the difference that changing language can subsequently make to perception.

Challenging behaviour

When I was a child, I was continually accused of displaying challenging behaviour. As an adult, I've read extensively on the subject and feel at least somewhat reassured that what I thought as a child is vindicated by my research as an adult. I was perpetually made to feel that my behaviour was my fault, that it was a deliberate and malicious way of being that messed up everyone else's day. That I was the one who needed to sort it out, control myself and stop being such a nightmare child. The truth is, I had very little control over how my anxiety manifested itself, and I didn't have the voice to communicate what I was so distressed about. Nowadays, I read about meltdowns, and how they are not a deliberate or conscious process – I wish folk knew about these things before they leapt on me to restrain

*me, and then spent endless (it seemed) amounts of energy
trying to stop me from ever behaving like that again. The
problem was that without those expulsions of energy, my
distress would have built and built until it manifested
in a far more dramatic and damaging way. I am not at
all convinced that I had what they called challenging
behaviour. And I can pretty much guarantee that however
annoying or difficult others found my behaviour at the
time, it was trivial compared to the distress that I was in.
I understand that now there is more of a view that all,
or much, behaviour can be communicative. Not that my
behaviour was a deliberate form of communication – in
fact, I was too out of control of my own behaviour for me
to think of it as communication; but it still said something.
Back then it said that I was challenging; I wonder, if I was
a child in today's more understanding society, whether
those same behaviours would be seen as communicating
distress. And, if so, whether something productive might
have been done instead of quite overtly child-shaming and
forcing me to believe that me and my behaviour were the
problem, not their lack of understanding.*

Selective mute

*I've always been labelled as being a 'selective mute' and
it's always stressed me out no end. What is selective about
being so anxious that I can't speak? Where is the choice
in that? Why is it that the wording itself suggests that it's
my choice, and that if only I made a bit more of an effort
then I could freely speak? Don't you think I want to have
a voice? In fact, it's more than just my imagination that
prompts these questions. I've been told, in no uncertain
terms. 'We know you can talk; your parents have told us,
so there's no excuse' – it's not an excuse, trust me. I have
no option at times. It's pretty simple – the more anxious*

I am, the more effort it takes to speak. And past a point of anxiety, I am unable to speak. My voice simply doesn't work, it shuts down. It is the equivalent of a gag. Try gagging a person and then telling them that because you heard them speak another time, there is no excuse not to speak now and see how far you get. It's the same for me; anxiety is my gag, so you telling me over and over that you know I can speak won't make it happen. I believe that you could perfectly justifiably label me as being situationally mute – that it is the situation that causes my inability to speak. I think that this would change everything for me. No longer would I be the problem, no longer would the blame be parked at my door. No longer would I be the one who has all the responsibility for 'selecting not to talk'. No longer would it be down to me to sort it all out. Perhaps others would take responsibility, try to work out what dreadful situation I am being exposed to that is so distressing that I am forced into being mute. Maybe then I wouldn't be so much at risk of being exposed to those dreadful situations, and I could finally regain my precious voice.

School refuser

I swear if they call her that one more time ... well, actually, I can't swear on that because I know all too well that it is almost an inevitability. 'She's a school refuser'; 'if she continues like this, she'll have to go on the school refuser register'; 'we take a zero-tolerance stance for school refusers so she will be facing exclusion unless she comes to school'; and so on, and so on. She's not refusing school, like it's a wilful choice on her behalf. School has created such a terrifying space that she is simply unable to force herself to face it. And, to be fair, I don't blame her one bit, which is why there is no way I will be trying to make her access school until such a time when they accept that they are the problem, and not my lovely daughter. They can put her on the register if they really want to. I mean, really. A register shaming children who, in the main, are neurodivergent children being scared stiff by their schools to the point of no return. Could we have a register of schools that are so autism-unfriendly that they create feelings of terror in our children?

Difficult child
Apparently, I was a difficult child. This is according to the psychologists – and there were lots of them. I was never labelled as difficult by my parents – maybe that's because, being autistic themselves, they fully appreciated why I was how I was, and secretly thought that what others viewed as difficult was, to them, perfectly logical. It seems that doing anything that in any way goes against the 'norm' leads to chances of being labelled as difficult. What happened to 'variety is the spice of life'? Honestly, where would we be if we were all the same? And being different should not be synonymous with being difficult. It's not like I'm doing it on purpose ...

Professional understanding

Communication options are a right

I was amazed the first time I accessed support for my child: amazed that there were no choices available for my child to be heard, amazed that no one really seemed that interested in what her perspective was, amazed at just how differently she was treated compared to other kids of her age who were able to speak. Just because she didn't have a verbal voice didn't mean that she didn't have a voice, an opinion or something worthy to communicate. And yet she was never given any option but to be – pardon the pun – silenced. Even when she was in the room, all communication directly involving her was directed at me: 'what would she like …?' and so on. I can't imagine what it must have been like for her in those days, being made invisible just because she had no verbalization. I love the fact that there are so many more options on offer now, that speaking is seen as just one aspect of communication, that children's voices are being heard without them speaking. I just wish that could have been the case for my child all those years ago; I wonder what difference it would have made to her fragile self-esteem if professionals had made the effort to hear her …

Autism understanding needs to reflect autistic children's needs

One single professional can make all the difference in the universe – and it makes me so sad to have to report that. It's a bit like those adverts about teaching, where we are told that 'everyone remembers a good teacher' or some such rhetoric. The ads are supposed to be inspiring, to get people to think about teaching as a career. That's fine. What I find deeply depressing is that they are so true; we do remember that teacher, mostly because they stand out. Logic dictates then, that all of the other teachers were not up to scratch. I'm sorry to say that it's even more apparent in the autism field. Finding that one professional who has the autism knowledge to actually make an effective difference to your child based on their needs is so hard because they are very few and far between. It is so wearing to keep knocking on doors, only to find that the lovely, well-meaning professional with a genuine desire to help has outdated 'knowledge' or believes that the solution they stumbled on that worked for another child will

be just as applicable to ours. Finding that one professional –
who, by the way, is almost inevitably a parent themselves and/
or an autistic adult – is worth so much; and yet it's just so rare.

Professionals understand that autism is not a mental health condition

Well, it isn't. I'm not quite sure if I need to elaborate – but I do
know that it's essential to point out. Too many professionals
are led to believe that autism is some kind of 'condition'
related to mental health, as opposed to a neurological way of
being that happens to differ in relation to the majority. The
fact that living as an autistic person then increases the risk of
mental health conditions – that's a separate point ...

Mental health conditions should be considered as potentially environmental and, therefore, could be alleviated outside of medication

Some children might have mental ill health as a primary
'condition' in the same way that anyone can be depressed, or
experience other mental health conditions. But most autistic
children experiencing depression are like that because of
the way in which they are misunderstood, or because the
environment around them is not suited to their needs. In those
cases, we would suggest that it is far more effective to work
on those environmental factors, rather than assuming that
medication is the best and only solution.

Therapy is adapted to meet autistic need

Going on from the point above, be aware that traditional
therapy with quite prescriptive methods may not suit autistic
children very well at all. Sometimes, in fact, therapy without
taking autism into consideration makes things worse. It is
pretty much essential to adapt therapy to have any chance
of it being beneficial to autistic people or children. Actually,

while we are on the subject – those people who have had the chance to access autistic therapists suggests that there would be mileage in developing a network of autistic therapists supporting autistic clients; it certainly works well for some autistic people, that's for sure.

Being autistic should not preclude support in any other area

We've just heard back from our local mental health support unit. 'Support' – that's a joke. I have the letter right here – I'm shaking so much I can barely read it; or maybe I just wish I hadn't read it in the first place. I am just so incredulous, incensed, angry, disappointed, but in the main just so devastated for my daughter. It's in plain black and white – 'we are advised that we should not be taking on autistic clients at present as they do not fit the remit of our service'. I mean, I actually can barely take it in. What level of absolute inadequacy can drive a service which purports to support individuals with poor mental health to exclude an entire population 'just' for being autistic? It absolutely beggars belief, but here is the letter to prove it. Quite aside from irony of the fact that it is the autistic population who are crying out (pun intended) for support around their mental health, what about the totally overt level of discrimination to refuse to allow access?

A few minutes later …

Ok, I've not calmed down. In fact, I don't think I could have felt any worse, but I carried on reading the letter. Not only is she denied a service because she's autistic, apparently, she wouldn't benefit anyway; allow me to quote again: 'while we are currently not taking on autistic clients, we would advise that your daughter's presentation of pathological anxiety fits the criteria of an

Autistic Spectrum Disorder so it is inadvisable to continue seeking support in this area ...' – what? Are they seriously suggesting that just because my daughter is autistic then she just has to put up with being pathologically anxious?

I feel that I should note, both of the above examples are based on real-life events.

Behaviour needs to be understood within an autism context

We shudder to think what might have happened had the clinician not had a degree of expertise on autism. We had previously been told, by someone else, that our son's 'presentation' fit the diagnostic criteria both for Obsessive Compulsive Disorder (OCD) and for anorexia. We could see why they suggested it and, when we looked up the 'symptoms' of these things, we also recognized the similarities. However, we were still a little dubious, and we are just so glad that we sought a second opinion. While she told us that OCD and anorexia could not be ruled out, she did note that there may be an alternative explanation to his behaviours. She explained all about how intense anxiety can manifest itself in different ways, and that it wasn't uncommon for autistic young people to feel very anxious because of their needs not being met. And that those anxieties can lead to the need for what appears to be control over certain aspects of life. She explained about the need for stability and that if a young person feels very unstable in one area of life, they might need to develop activities that make them feel more control in others. She explained that our son's intensified routines and stricter impositions on his eating habits might be manifestations of the need for stability, born out of anxiety – rather than what might traditionally be understood as OCD and anorexia.

Sensory profiles

Sensory profiles and audits must be ongoing and up to date

Having a sensory profile is an essential component in understanding any autistic person. Having a full understanding of how the sensory world (internal and external) might impact a person is invaluable as it helps one understand the lived experiences – of self, or others. By internal, I mean aspects such as interoception; by external, I mean the factors outside of the body such as noise. I've written in most of my books about sensory issues, so there is no need to go through it all again here. But in terms of the suggested adjustment, my point is that without a sensory profile, surely there is a strong argument that there is less of a chance that a person's needs will be met. In essence, there is a very strong possibility that without a sensory profile, there won't be the knowledge of what might need to be done to reduce discrimination. However, while sensory profiles are becoming more common, what is also necessary is the subsequent implementation of what needs to be done once a sensory profile has been developed. In other words, there is little point in having a sensory profile, however good it is, unless subsequent action is taken. (Actually, a quick caveat – a sensory profile is extremely important when it comes to sense and understanding of self.) However, for the purpose of this adjustment, it is the combination of the profile and the audit that is the goal. Having an audit of the environment in which the individual accesses *against the individual sensory profile* is, so far as I can tell, the *only* way to identify what adjustments in the sensory environment should be made specific to that person. A sensory profile on its own without an audit and subsequent action is not enough.

Accident and emergency

A & E settings are usually autism-unfriendly; provide alternatives where possible

I think that it's fair to suggest that not many people really like Accident and Emergency departments, possibly because, if you are there, you or a loved one is probably in some level of problematic health-related situation. However, for many reasons, not least sensory ones, accessing A & E can make matters even worse for the autistic person. I am no expert on A & E departments and how they operate, but some of my students who have shared their experiences – both as autistic people accessing A & E and as staff who work in A & E – have noted just how discriminatory they might potentially be. After all, if you cannot even enter a ward without fear of sensory overload at a time when your anxiety is likely to be heightened anyway, surely this could place you at a substantial disadvantage. One of my students told me of an amazing practice at her hospital in which, where possible, knowing an autistic patient was coming in via car or ambulance, they made every effort to at least initially see the person in the car park to avoid them having to come into the A & E department. What a fantastic adjustment.

Fabricated or induced illness

Research on Fabricated or Induced Illness (FII) is imperative

This was going to feature as a bigger part of this book until I remembered that it was supposed to be about reasonable adjustments, not a discourse on the incredible travesties of justice that I am aware of concerning allegations against autistic parents of autistic children around Fabricated or

Induced Illness. I will be writing about this more extensively in the next book specific to adults. In the meantime, suffice to suggest that I fully support the idea of properly funded, participatory and emancipatory research into FII and autism, which should be considered, seriously, as a reasonable adjustment.

9

Bits and bobs

- All autistic children have access to animals
- Easy access is provided to outdoor spaces
- Bicycles and cycle trailers are free to use
- Obsessions are renamed as passionate interests
- Passionate interests are recognized for the joy they bring and are not vilified just because of their topic
- Children are allowed/encouraged to explore passionate interests within education
- Queues don't exist for those who can't use them
- Food/drink can be brought with you
- Seats can be chosen and pre-booked on rides
- Numbers of goes on a ride can be organized in advance, and children can stay on a ride without having to queue up again

Pets/animals

Never underestimate just how glorious animals are, and the necessity for some autistic children to engage with animals. Many autistic children will have an empathic response to animals that is far greater – not than their empathy with humans, but compared to non-autistic empathy with animals. The relationship between child and [insert species here] can be the difference between survival and the alternative for some – that is how important it is. It doesn't matter whether you are a family who is able to have pets; access to animals is absolutely an adjustment that I feel is reasonable to request:

All autistic children have access to animals

I literally cannot live on a day-to-day basis without organizing my entire existence around thinking about the last time I saw my turtle and thinking about when I am next going to see him (I think it's a 'him'; I'm not quite sure, though). I've been told that most people don't have such an attachment, which I find bewildering – but irrelevant. They are the ones who are missing out, after all. I'm the one who has the most incredible, beautiful, joyous companion who never judges me, is always happy to see me, shares all the things I want to talk about, and gives me more comfort than anyone in the whole universe (sorry, Mum and Dad – but what's true is true; you two are ok, but you're not turtles). People ask me why turtle is so special. They also ask me why he (she?) hasn't got a name. They very often ask the two questions essentially simultaneously, which I sort of find amusing. I'm never quite sure what to tell them, because when I try to explain in my own way how important turtle is they clearly don't understand. I think it's a frame of reference thing. I mean, if they already know how deliciously fantastic turtle was, then presumably they wouldn't need to ask. And because they need to ask, they probably won't understand the answer. I want to say, Why does it matter? Why can't you just accept how important he (she?) is? And when it comes to naming, well – he (she?) doesn't belong to me. The whole idea of ownership of an animal disgusts me. He (she?) is simply with me, sort of on loan. It's not my role to impose a name on him (her?) and anyway, as I don't speak turtle, any name would be meaningless. Also, as you may have noticed, I don't really know what gender it is anyway ...

I honestly think that funding in all authorities (which, presumably, would be minimal) for all children to have access to animals would be a reasonable adjustment. Not only for the companionship but also for learning opportunities. Schools should keep chickens, have ponds with tadpoles and have a friendly rat or three (no singletons, please – we don't want lonely rats).

Nature

Easy access is provided to outdoor spaces

Part of the reason why I love the remote outdoors is the lack of people noise – and, to be fair, the lack of people! I like nature noise – revel in it, in fact – but people noise makes my skin crawl. I don't think it's their voices per se, it's the association I have with them. The fact that I associate voices almost entirely with negativity – being told off, being bullied, being made to feel worthless, being corrected – all of those things build up and build up to the point where any voice at all has the capability of sending me spinning into a cycle of despondency that I find it very difficult to extricate myself from. However, the new scheme in my city is to provide free transport for those eligible and the bus drops folk off at pre-booked stops of their choosing for a specific duration. This means that I can pretty much guarantee that I can chill out with Mum for a couple of hours in the forest without any chance of being triggered. It is genuinely a part of the week that I don't think I could do without. Somehow, I feel that having those two hours means that I can process all the rubbish that I've endured over the past week and get myself ready to face the following week. It might sound like not much to many people, but for me it's two hours of irreplaceable joy.

Bicycles and cycle trailers are free to use

Well, where to start? My kid simply loves movement, loves the feeling of forward momentum, loves being able to relax in the wind. She can't yet ride a bike, but we discovered a bike hire centre just out of town that had a circuit going around a lake. The council have started a new initiative – I think it was all about trying to get folk outdoors and a bit fitter, I'm not really sure. What I do know is that it's made quite an extraordinary difference to our family. We don't have much in the way of spare cash, and what we do have is spent mainly on climbing equipment for our small garden – she is forever climbing on stuff and our garden looks a bit like a kids' play area! But what we didn't have was a space for her to really feel ongoing movement – when at home, she uses her slide, but even that isn't enough. This new initiative has made all the difference in the world. Every day, rain or shine, after school, we divert our journey and do a lap of the lake with her sat all comfy in the trailer. A single lap of the lake and she's super happy to go home. It used to be the case that the transition between school and home caused her so much difficulty – now, though, the lap around the lake seems to break the transition up and provide her some much-needed regulation time to prepare her for going home. We used to spend all evening chasing her around the garden trying to get her ready for bed; it's made the biggest difference in the world. I wish I could show you the videos of before and after – you just wouldn't believe what an impact a bike ride could have. Mind you, I'm looking forward to the day that she learns to ride herself!

Passionate interests

Obsessions are renamed as passionate interests

*'I'm afraid your son is displaying signs of obsessive
behaviour' – I remember the words as if they were
yesterday, and I shudder just as much today as I did
18 years ago. It was after we had been called into school
to discuss the school's 'concerns' – as reflected in the
words they used in the meeting. It was all 'afraid' this and
'apprehensive' that – I won't repeat the more negative
ones, but I remember at the time thinking 'this is my son
you're talking about, could you perhaps be a little less
negative about who he is?' Honestly, I'm glad you weren't
there to hear it, you'd have wept inwardly too. As a family
we had never had a single problem – until he went to
school. From that day on he 'became' a problem – though
for the life of me, I could never really figure out what the
actual problem was. He was quirky, for sure – but then so
am I and so is his dad, and we love quirkiness. In fact, we
sometimes worry that non-quirky folk are missing out to a
large degree. To then be informed that there were whole-
school 'concerns' over – in this case – apparent 'obsessive
behaviour' really was a blow. I felt a bit bad about it, but
I did have to confess in that very meeting a number of
things, not least that I also would fit into their definition
of obsessive behaviour, that I had a very successful career
as a direct result of it, and that I was probably part of
the perceived problem as I had always encouraged his
level of focus on whatever it was that interested him as
a pre-school child. I'm not quite sure what they thought
about it all, but they did seem a little put out that I wasn't
really buying into their 'intervention' of restricting his
interests. Anyway, sitting here in the graduation hall*

waiting for my son to be presented with his PhD certificate along with his inspirational student award for being one of the university's youngest ever doctoral students, I feel somewhat vindicated that I took him out of the school system and encouraged him to be as obsessive as he wanted to be.

Passionate interests are recognized for the joy they bring and are not vilified just because of their topic

It's a weird one; I have to be super careful about what I share and with whom. It doesn't seem to matter that I am so passionate about certain things, but I have learned the hard way to check with a trusted source as to whether my current passion is 'appropriate'. I don't know what the exact definition of society's perspective on 'appropriate' actually is, and that can cause me so many problems. I have had – literally – dozens of passions over my lifetime, all of which give me equal joy, so long as I am left to pursue those passions at my own pace and in my own space. Long school holidays in which I can really let myself loose are pure joy; the knowledge that Mum and Dad let me immerse myself fully in whatever subject area I'm interested in at the time makes me the happiest person alive – or, at least, that's what it feels like. I can't imagine not being motivated to learn about something new; and yet when I have been told that I am not 'supposed' to be interested in whatever my current passion is, it's like a physical blow. I literally have had to mourn a subject and have only been rescued by promises from my parents that I can continue with my passion, just without sharing it with teachers at school. I mean, I'm not stupid – I'm fully aware that there are restrictions around the scope of my learning based on my age, and that's fine. I'm a bit like the characters in Hogwarts who, when they are granted permission, get to read books out of the restricted section of the library. I don't mind restrictions based on my age. What I resent – and 'resent' is far too mild a word – is when I get restricted by school just because of the topic. I've been told all sorts, from 'that's something boys shouldn't be interested in' (a comment made to me in primary school when I was passionate about the history of dolls) to 'you shouldn't be looking up disgusting things like that' (again in primary school when I was interested in scientific dissection in the Victorian age) all the way through to 'it's concerning that you are displaying these interests' (a secondary school project that I wanted to write on serial killers). What I find interesting is that most of the areas I've been passionate about have gone down really well – I've done so many presentations at school on, for example, how best to keep bees, why Einstein was so important, and the history of the climate change movement. To me, all learning is valuable, irrespective of the topic. I am fully aware that men have made fortunes designing dolls, that there can be brilliant careers in science that include investigating the insides of people, and that learning about serial killers is an important component of understanding the human race – but, according to school, 'safer' topics are the only ones that I am supposed to be passionate about.

Children are allowed/encouraged to explore passionate interests within education

I spent so many years at school with very little motivation – which led to very poor 'performances' when it came to grades, exams, coursework, you name it. I had the label of being a sub-par achiever, and expectations of me were pretty much rock bottom. Sadly, even I bought into the notion that I was educationally useless. It wasn't until much, much later as an adult that I became aware that it wasn't that I was intellectually inferior – which was the inference (actually, on occasion, it wasn't an inference – it was an overt accusation/comment directed towards me which really doesn't do a child's confidence much good whatsoever) when in school. What I didn't realize was the link – for me at least – between interest, motivation and academic achievement. If I am interested in something, I then have massive motivation to pursue it – which, as it happens, has led to academic achievement. Luckily, I was given an amazing opportunity when a university 'allowed' me to take a Master's degree pursuing my area of interest, and such was the success of that, I followed it up with a PhD – which, ironically, perhaps, I found easier than any of the subjects I was tasked with at school. It does make me wonder, though, if I had been allowed to include my subject of interest within the curriculum subjects, what that might have led to.

This is based on real events. What I have also found is that if education allows – even encourages – passionate interests as part of the learning process, then all sorts can be achieved. 'Write a story which includes an explanation of your use of verbs and adjectives' – compared to 'write a story about lighthouses which includes an explanation of your use of verbs and adjectives'. I know this sounds ridiculously simple, but you might be astounded at the influence this can have (by the way, this is also based on a real event and the impact was huge).

Theme parks

It's not something that you tend to think about in relation to autism and reasonable adjustments, but I've chosen to include theme parks in the book just as a reminder that outside of the more 'traditional' areas of childhood, there are also all sorts of places and environments where, as an autistic child, you might be at a substantial disadvantage if reasonable adjustments are not made. I've suggested a small number here, just as examples of things that can be done to properly include autistic children in everyday living in a way that is their right.

Queues don't exist for those who can't use them

I honestly think that this is one of those areas where if you don't suffer from it then you refuse to believe that it's actually a very real thing. By which I mean I've had so many comments over the years telling me that I am 'using my autism' 'as an excuse not to queue'. I'm not 'using my autism' in any way, shape or form. The simple fact is that having to queue would immediately discount my ability to access the ride. I literally cannot queue. Well, maybe that's an exaggeration. I could, I suppose, be forced to queue; in fact, I was introduced to 'gradual queueing' at school where I was subjected to having to wait for things with a countdown timer which had an extra 10 seconds added to it each time I underwent the process. It was – and this is literal – agony. The inertia and having to wait is emotionally agonizing. And trust me when I say I would choose physical agony over emotional agony any time. The emotional pain that I suffer when having to queue is such that there are very few things in life that are so important that would balance it out. Enjoyment, for example, is nothing compared to emotional pain. I would easily forgo enjoyment in order to avoid emotional pain – every time. What that means, of course, is that I often have to choose not to enjoy myself, which to be honest seems a bit harsh – especially when the solution is just to let me go to the front of the queue. To me it seems absolutely reasonable to sacrifice one place in a queue of people if that means that a child can enjoy the exact same thing that everyone else takes for granted. As I've stated, though, if you don't suffer from emotional pain when queueing, you just appear to pretend that it doesn't exist.

Food/drink can be brought with you

I guess it must be a tough business, theme parks. And I also guess that financially the catering aspect of theme parks is an important one, and that they probably make a good chunk of their profits on catering, which is fair enough. The trouble is, unless my child is allowed to bring his own food and drink, we can't go to the theme park. It's as simple as that. Surely it's reasonable, then, for us as a family to bring his food and drink and then for the rest of us to access the catering the same as everyone else? All it takes is for us to have a different colour wrist band so that security doesn't constantly want to kick us out for feeding our child, who can only eat food that he knows he has prepared himself. The alternative being that the theme park misses out on all our tickets, and we miss out on the theme park.

Choice of seat that can be pre-booked on rides

I am so excited to finally be able to ride on the one I've been waiting for – I've been waiting for years, and have spent so many hours queueing up only to be disappointed over and over again. I even tried to work out some kind of system to make sure that when it was my turn I could go straight to the front of the ride, but despite being close it never happened, and I had to leave it for another time. I've tried to explain to people why it's so important for me to be at the front, and I think they sympathize with me, but it still doesn't help. You see, the thought of being behind anyone on a ride like this fills me with so much dread that I just can't do it. The thought of the bodily fluids that could leak out of a person in front of me, and those fluids hitting me in the face at considerable speed is enough to make me gag. And if it happened in reality, I suspect that I would not just gag – it would be an eruption that would haunt not just me but everyone else on the ride forever! So I just have to miss out; or, at least, I did, until the new system came into play. I can now go online and pre-book the front seat; all they do is get a notification when I arrive in the queue, and when they know that it will be my turn next, they just reserve the front seat for me, irrespective as to where I am in the queue. It's so simple, and yet absolute genius – and I can finally achieve my ambition.

Numbers of goes on a ride can be organized in advance, and children can stay on a ride without having to queue up again

I am absolutely blown away at what I've just read on the theme park's website – in fact, it's so astonishingly cool that I will simply share it with you; here it is:

We are aware that some of you with neurodivergent children might struggle to access some of our rides. We are also aware that we are limited in what we can do to be inclusive, so would welcome your suggestions. One such suggestion by a parent has led to us to introduce a new system which might suit your family. This all came about because once this particular child was on a ride, he found it almost impossible to get off; there were 'scenes' shall we say, and our staff and the child were all left rather distressed. One of the things that the child is very good at is understanding limits – we were told that if he knows that he has, for example, three goes on a ride then he will accept it, no problem. But he doesn't logically see why he can't stay on the ride while it goes around three times. He also needs a physical reminder of the number of goes he has been allocated, and his parents have informed us that he won't accept the number limitation from them – it has to come from staff at the theme park. So – we are very pleased to announce that we have introduced a token system, whereby (with advance discussion) we will provide, for example, three tokens when your child gets on the ride. Each time the ride is complete, a staff member will take one token. When the tokens are gone, it is time to get off the ride. We are absolutely aware that this 'solution' might only work for a small number of families, which is why we would love it if you used the comment section below to add other ideas that we might consider for future inclusive practice.

Conclusions

In a sense, I find it extraordinary that a book needs to be written based on the mind-blowing fact that autistic children are so hard done by when it comes to discrimination. I'm not sure why, in this day and age, they are a population that is so unrepresentative when it comes to proper inclusion and equity. The adults who share their lives with me so often identify their difficult childhoods as critical precursors to long-term problems. We know this. We know that difficult times as a child often lead to difficult times as an adult. We know that autistic wellbeing as an adult is not as common as it should be. We know that something needs to be done.

But this book is about optimism, not pessimism.

I mention microaggressions earlier on in the book, and am filled with optimism. While there is a long way to go in almost all areas of discrimination, there has been considerable progress over the years, which demonstrates that things *can* change. I delight in the motto created by Antonio Gramsci: 'pessimism of the intellect, optimism of the will'. Just because we are aware of the problematic times that our intellect tells us exist doesn't mean that we can't optimistically strive for better. I hope that this book can play some small part in the journey towards happy autistic children.

Index